SING
IN THE NIGHT

Going through the Iron gates of emotional
prison into peace

SING
IN THE NIGHT

PAMELA R. GARIN

TATE PUBLISHING
AND ENTERPRISES, LLC

Published by Tate Publishing & Enterprises, LLC
127 E. Trade Center Terrace | Mustang, Oklahoma 73064 USA
1.888.361.9473 | www.tatepublishing.com

Tate Publishing is committed to excellence in the publishing industry. The company reflects the philosophy established by the founders, based on Psalm 68:11,
"The Lord gave the word and great was the company of those who published it."

Book design copyright © 2016 by Tate Publishing, LLC. All rights reserved.
Cover design by Nino Carlo Suico
Interior design by Gram Telen

Published in the United States of America
ISBN: 978-1-68118-200-1
Religion / Christian Ministry / Preaching
16.06.06

1

Origin of Pain

The man grew up in a small Illinois town and was raised during the Great Depression. As a boy, he was a decent human being, loyal to country and family.

He served in the US navy and saw active combat in WWII. The man raised four children and was a Boy Scout leader. He was faithful to his wife, faithful to his job, and supportive to his friends. The man's hobby was woodworking. He taught his children the value of hard work and discipline. He was a strict disciplinarian and seemed to practice what he preached. When the man was in his sixties, he divorced his wife and moved over a thousand miles away from the place he raised his family. He remarried sometime in the 1980s, and for all outward appearances, most of his life, he seemed to have an easygoing manner and friendly disposition. As the years progressed, the man's easygoing manner began to deteriorate. Angry outbursts about insignificant subjects became more and more frequent. As the years went by, the angry outbursts morphed into periods of rage. This man, who for most of his life seemed easygoing and happy, would now spit out long monologues of large and small past hurts and injustices with so much rage that you thought the incidents had just happened. His patient demeanor slowly gave way to an impatient attitude that would manifest itself in a tirade of four-letter words peppered with bigotry and hate. The last years of his life, one by one, the man had little or no relationship with his children. As a mother, it was difficult to hear the names he would call his own children. The accusations of their "supposed" misdeeds, to us, seemed unreasonable in the extreme. We all think his "new" wife had some part in the anger and unrest as it was apparent that she wished all the inheritance to go to her daughter instead of the man's children. This, she accomplished. He hated me too, although I never knew why. He never told me what he thought I had done or omitted, he was just rude, crude, and sometimes downright mean, but I comforted myself with the thought that I had not seen him treat his own children much better. Once he assaulted me with four-letter words just because I had mentioned that I was thinking of buying sheep. In between the curse words, I got the message that I was stupid, just like the sheep. He thought that anything as personal as his relationship with God was no one else's business, and if you asked him about it, he would fly into yet another rage and scream about foxholes in WWII under heavy fire where he "got it right" with God. He would point his finger at you and dare you to try and talk to him about it any further. Intimidation became a way of life for him. More years passed and the man's fits of rage sometimes gave way to long periods of depression. The man's smiles became less, his tirades were more frequent, and his friends were fewer. At the age of eighty-two, after arguing with his wife in the kitchen, the man, my father-in-law, calmly walked into the bedroom, held a pistol to his head and ended his life. What happened? Who thinks like this? What was the rage really about? What was the real reason for his anger and subsequent choice of death? Was this a perfect picture of post–traumatic stress disorder, born in a foxhole in WWII? Or was this something equally as traumatic? Maybe this was a combination of hurtful incidents known only to him.

Only God knows the real answer to these questions, but whatever the answer is, I am convinced that too many of us in this world can relate. Too many past hurts with no resolutions. Too many past traumatic events with no healing. Pain and suffering kept deep inside of us because even the telling of the incidents is too horrible. Dark holes in the recesses of our souls that words cannot express. Dark holes in our souls that we are afraid to express. For some, the only comfortable way to deal with the darkness is with rage and anger. Why is it that, the answers to pain are not so readily available? If they are easily available, why have so many of us missed it? Why is there so much dysfunction and unrest in a world where material objects are so plentiful? What has happened to so many of us? If I had not heard the voice of God in my life at age thirteen, this could have been me, and I wonder if I would even have lasted to the age of thirty. Three PhD psychologists said that these negative anger issues should be part of my life. They said that I should not be functioning at all and suffer with multiple personality disorder, but marveled that I not only function, but function well and have no sign of MPD. At the tender age of five years old, I was abducted by a Satan-worshiping coven and brutally raped and tortured. At the age of five, I had no way of expressing my horror to my parents or anyone else. Are there really words in the English language that can adequately express these horrors? I could not find nor express them. I suppressed my pain and memories as best as I could and never thought that the trauma that I experienced would affect me any further, but it did. Poor choices, no self esteem, no sense of security, obsessive compulsive disorder, and other negative things in my life were direct results of what I suffered at five years old.

It was not until I was thirty-five years old that I sought professional treatment. My torture was so severe that I had difficulty even finding a therapist that would work with me. Too often, after a few sessions, the therapist would apologetically tell me he could not help me because "they never taught me how to deal with this in school." I kept hearing that they were sorry and did not know what to do with someone so incredibly damaged. They all wanted to know how I could be functioning so normally, given my horrible past circumstances. I told them that it must be the grace of God that sustained me. I did manage to find some help, but most of the healing that I enjoy today came from what I learned in the Bible. In the Word of God, I found the answers of how to heal, how to be productive, and how to make deep wounds and hurt into painless scars. I discovered that healing is basically a series of obedient actions to God, and all the actions are manageable by anyone. Wounds are painful, scars are not. Scars are just a reminder of trauma, but are no longer painful because healing has occurred. I was diagnosed post–traumatic stress disorder (PTSD), but nightmares, flashbacks, and other problems associated with PTSD are for the most part ended. The last psychologist that I saw about 1995 was smiling when he informed me that I need not spend my money to see him anymore as I was well indeed. He told me that I may still encounter problems with triggers and self-esteem, but I could manage that without his help. If I did need him, he was available, but I have not seen him since that time. The unusual aspect of this previous conversation was the fact that but for a bit of guidance and encouragement, he really did not have that much to do with my healing, and because this man is a Christian, he knew that.

My healing came about by learning certain truths in the Bible and being willing to obey what the Word of God said. I did not have to wait for certain circumstances to change or certain bad feelings to go away. I learned that I could start to feel better almost immediately if I made the correct biblical choices. I could choose to heal instead of waiting endlessly for all the negatives to go away. Everyone who has been traumatized wants all the negative issues and feelings to disappear. And I think that everyone who has ever been traumatized wants and expects all the negative issues to go away with no effort at all. Healing takes effort. You must make a firm decision to heal and then choose to do whatever it takes to get there. I think most people are not unwilling to do what it takes to heal, they just don't know where to start or how to continue on. What I will show you is a systematic approach to healing that makes a very painful process more manageable. Today, I am happy to report that my self-esteem is pretty healthy and my whole life has improved by what I have learned and applied.

When I was trying to figure out how to heal, I looked for a book like the one I am writing now, but could not find one. I wanted a book written by someone who had suffered severe trauma and had gained victory over all the negative aspects. I wanted more than just a tell-all that told me everything about their experience, but gave me few personal workable solutions. I wanted to be told what practical things I could do, with a step-by-step approach, so that I could gauge my progress and feel as if I was accomplishing something. This book is what I was looking for, and my prayer is that my experience coupled with the solutions that I found can help you. The first truth that I recognized is that I must, of course, ask God to heal me, then I must give Him permission to do so. We all need to give the Lord permission to come into our lives and heal us. If God automatically healed us from all our pains, then the whole world would be healed, would it not? I learned that the Lord is patiently waiting there for us to ask Him to come into our lives and intervene in our sorrows. We all have a free will. As a survivor that has sat in many hours of group therapy, I observed that generally people will ask God to heal them. They want God to heal them, but they do not want to give Him the permission to come into their lives and change and then do what it takes to get them completely healed. I think that many people do not obtain healing in their lives simply because they subconsciously feel they have a right (because of their trauma) to hang on to all of their grief, pain, and sorrow instead of taking that first step to give God the right and permission to begin to heal all their hurts. Giving God permission means to be willing to work with Him to do whatever it takes to change whatever it takes so that we can obtain complete healing and a truly happy and blessed life.

Action Assignment

1. Read Psalm 107:13–43. Think about crying to the Lord and his provision,

2. Pray and give God permission to begin to overhaul your life and heal all of your sorrows. Read 2 Chronicles 20:20–22.

3. Read Philippians 4:13. Remember that in spite of uncomfortable circumstances, you *can* do the tasks.

2

I Am Not Alone

Over the decades, I have talked to countless survivors of trauma, and one of the most prevalent feelings of frustration is the feeling that you are alone. No one understands, no one gets it. Before we can get into the conversations that address the practical things we can do to heal, I think it is necessary to address the feelings of isolation that we who have survived intense trauma feel. It is difficult to sit opposite a therapist that only knows your pain from a textbook. I believe that it was more difficult for me to heal because of that incredible feeling that the person sitting opposite me "just does not get it." I did not feel understood. I felt that no one has ever suffered as intensely as I had, and no one would ever understand, therefore, no one could help me. I know that these are common feelings among those of us who have survived. This short chapter will address that, so that we can move on to the real aspects of healing and being well emotionally.

> Heal me, O Lord, and I shall be healed; save me, and I shall be saved: for thou art my praise. (Jeremiah 17:14)

Making a victim of trauma feel isolated is a primary tool of the devil to keep you in bondage to the pain. Then you can relive the trauma over and over again, thus preventing you from having a wonderful life. The word of God is full of examples of people who endured great trauma, and the most amazing example of this is, of course, Jesus the Christ. None of us has suffered as much intense pain as he has. When I was beginning my healing journey, this truth was my starting point. I know I am not alone because Christ has suffered more, and I am not the only child that has been abducted—I am not alone.

The suffering of Jesus as our starting point will give way to the next frustration that survivor's experience, and that is the annoying instant replay. In any traumatic or hurtful experience, stopping the brain from replaying the event can be as easy a herding cats or giving your mother-in-law advice. Whether the pain you have is minor, such as a stinging barb of insult by a coworker or major trauma of abuse and loss, getting your mind to stop replaying the event is like battling a wildfire. Just when you think you have some headway, the wind picks up, fans the flames, and you feel as if you have accomplished nothing.

Our brains are built with the ability to memorize, and this is the one time that the natural function of the brain works against you. For those of us who have suffered pain, the frustration is intense, as you experience the hurt all over again. Every feeling, every thought, every injustice, every anger is relived as if it were happening now. If you are PTSD, this suffering is even more intense and is referred to as "flashbacks." I do not suffer flashbacks anymore. If you can learn and apply the truths that I share with you, I think it very possible that if you are plagued with flashbacks, they may cease for you also. For me, the tools which I share throughout this writing are the things I believe eliminated my flashbacks. One day, I just noticed that I had not had a flashback in a very long time. As of this writing, I have not had a real flashback in over fifteen years. The experts said that is impossible for someone as traumatized as I was, but I am telling you the truth.

When you relive the trauma, by the time you get a handle on the memories and calm yourself down a bit, you are tired. Then, by the time you are finished reliving, you may be punishing yourself for the events that were not your fault, and you are in a very dark place emotionally.

At these times of sorrow, I felt a real kinship with Job.

> Let the day perish wherein I was born. (Job 3:3)

When I read on to verse 26, I thought it was really describing the dark place I was in. After the devil has done all the instant replays about my assaults, pain, and anger. I would get to go over every blow, every feeling, every loss, every injustice and I would begin to say of my birthday:

> Let darkness and the shadow of death stain it; let a cloud dwell upon it; let the blackness of the day terrify it. (Job 3:5)

This is a perfect picture of depression and the devil loves it.

Our heavenly Father does not want us in these dark places. God is not pleased when we have feelings of sadness and struggle with the past. I think that the inclusion of these passages of scripture proves that God understands our feelings. The Word of God states that he is touched with the feelings of our infirmities.

> For we have not an high priest which cannot be touched with the feeling of our infirmities: but was in all points tempted like as we are, yet without sin. (Hebrews 4:15)

This passage of scripture in Hebrews is, of course, referring to Jesus. He has suffered every bad thing that we have and more, He gets it! How comforting! No one else in the world may fully understand your pain, but Jesus does understand and has experienced your exact pain, you are not alone.

For all who are attempting to heal, this is our starting point. It is my belief that until we eradicate those feelings of being alone, we cannot fully heal. This is where we start. To get rid of the feelings of isolation is simple, we just believe and trust God that we are not alone and He understands. This is a simple act of will. I choose to acknowledge that God understands my pain and has not left me alone.

I choose to believe that Jesus has suffered everything that I have, and I am not the only one to experience this loss, pain, and frustration of trauma. I have someone to accompany me on my journey of healing!

On your healing adventure, this will be the easiest part. Unfortunately, the rest of your journey will take a bit more effort, and skipping steps will slow or stop your healing process. As you read each chapter, if you have to stop at that station for a while before you go on to the next chapters, it is okay. I would be surprised if you got it all quickly, and in the hours it may take you to read, your healing is complete. Take your time and work through each issue.

This is going to take a lot of effort on your part, but the rewards are good. This can be a new you and a new life if you commit to put forth the effort.

I once talked to a personal trainer, who was giving me a bunch of advice on how to lose my extra pounds and get in shape.

I know that she was telling the truth, but I could not help asking, "Do I have to do everything? Do I have to do all of these things?"

"No, you do not have to do everything. You just have to decide how fat you want to be."

What a wake-up! I am challenging you in the same way.

How healed do you want to be? How much life-crippling anger do you want to hold on to? How miserable do you really want to be? Is a little bit of dark days okay?

As I attempted to heal, it became apparent to me that I had more control over the misery than I had originally thought! Previously, I thought I was trapped and doomed to relive the junk for the rest of my life.

As you study and read about my healing journey, you will discover that you have more power than you think.

So the summary of this chapter is that to feel better we must first accept the truth that we are not alone in suffering, and second, we must accept the challenge to do whatever it takes to get there.

> Be careful for nothing; but in every thing by prayer and supplication with thanksgiving let you requests be made known unto God. And the peace of God which passes all understanding, shall keep your Hearts and minds through Christ Jesus. Those things which ye have both learned, and received, and heard, and seen in me, do: and the peace of God shall be with you. (Philippians 4: 6,7, 9)

Action Assignment

1. Decide to accept the fact that others have suffered in your similar manner.

2. Accept the fact that healing will require an attitude of "I can" and not the usual "I can't." Healing is really an act of the will, and obedience and this will be better understood as the steps progress.

3. Read over the highlighted scriptures in this chapter and believe.

4. Read 2 Chronicles 20:20–22.

5. Think about how much it helped the Israelites to sing and praise before they embarked on the war against their enemies.

6. Think about what kind of "singing gives us power over our pain and adversity," answer: it is praise to our God.

7. Singing (praising God) in times of trouble makes all the healing faster and easier. The key here is attitude.

8. Read Jeremiah 29:11–13.

Prayer

I thank you, Jesus, that you have made every provision for me to heal. I believe that it is your perfect will that I feel emotionally well and function at my highest level. Please give me the courage to do all that is required of me to heal, and I thank you that as you and I embark on this healing journey, that you will do for me the things I cannot, so that I can completely heal. Amen.

3

Close Your Eyes

I live with my husband, Mark, in the Rocky Mountains of Colorado. Ranching is ripe with life experiences that are similar to spiritual experiences. I often can live through something, then see a spiritual application. Maybe it is because I live three hours away from the mall! Obviously, with the kids grown and on their own as well as being so far from the mall, I have lots of time to think about everything. One of the most difficult attitudes for me to overcome was the attitude of mistrust. With the trauma that I endured, difficulty trusting God sometimes goes with the territory .Mistrust of man is expected, but God does not expect me to trust every person, just Him.

Mistrust can be victim thinking. With respect to trusting God, we can decide not to engage in victim thinking, but "how not to" can be a problem. God showed me "how" in a rather unique way.

It is a little known fact that I do not see too well in the dark. Apparently, I see well enough to pass my driver's exam, but not well enough to do my best driving after the sun goes down.

If I know the route well and it is well lit, I will confidently venture out. If not, I usually stay home and rerun the memories of Mark coming with the ranch truck to pull me out of some ditch that I had misjudged.

My less than perfect night vision causes more grief when I am out late with Mark at the wheel. He can see well, I cannot. That does not stop me from telling him to slow down, stop longer, don't go yet, or any other copilot demands that truly make him furious.

I tend to forget that, although the dark side of the mountain looks close to me, I do not see it as well as Mark sees it.

Instead of copilot feuding with my husband, I am learning to trust him. When we get in the car to take a night drive in an area I am unfamiliar with, I close my eyes.

When my eyes are open, I am trusting my vision.

When my eyes are closed, I am trusting Mark's vision. Mark's vision is more reliable.

Closing my eyes when Mark is driving at night has made our relationship much easier, but it was difficult for me to train myself to do.

When I have been caught out on horseback after dark, I have a bit of a panic and then give the horse his head, letting him be the driving control. I do not see too well in the dark, but horses do, so I always have to trust my horse to get me home and the horse has never let me down.

Trauma survivors tend to always have an intense need to see and sometimes an equally intense need to control a situation where all the facts are not seen clearly. This reasoning is a direct result of being a survivor. We do not want to be caught in a traumatic situation again, so we are on guard, protecting ourselves. This kind of reasoning makes us feel safer. After all, our trauma came about because of our inability to fully see and control our situation.

Eyes wide open and control is understandable and the best solution if you are walking out into a big parking lot alone, but not always the best solution for other matters.

If I am in an unfamiliar area by myself, such as a parking lot, mall, or restaurant, calmly paying attention to my surroundings is prudent. It matters little if you are male or female, it is just wise to be alert.

Sometimes, we just need to trust someone else out of necessity.

I cannot perform my own surgery or fill my own tooth. Sometimes, necessity dictates that we trust others. Survivors can often have a big problem with all aspects of trust. We have not had the pleasure to get to believe the lie called "it can't happen to me." If you are a survivor of incest, severe accident, robbery, rape, home invasion, abduction, or other trauma, you know it "can" happen. If you have had abusive parents, teachers, grandparents, coworkers, or spouses, you can be (and usually are) equally as traumatized. The feelings are the same.

I am not commanded of God to blindly trust everyone. In fact, my motto is that trust needs to be earned, not freely bestowed on everyone just because they "don't look like a criminal." What does a criminal look like anyway? My criminals were grandmotherly and young handsome men who talk nice and give ice cream to neighbor children. Who saw that coming?

I need not trust everyone. I have learned, however, that trusting God is something I need to do.

Of all the struggles I went through as I passed through the corridors of my healing journey, I took the longest time at the "trusting God" station!

Trusting God in every situation was the hardest thing for me to learn. Most of the toughest battles I have engaged in are when I know that trusting God is the smart thing to do, but convincing myself to exercise trust has been a bloody battle indeed.

This attitude can be, of course, traced back to when I was five years old and I was kidnapped. I used to think that if God allowed those monsters to kidnap me, I could not trust him much.

Sure, I lived through it (the trauma), but as any survivor knows, living with the pain sometimes feels worse than the initial trauma, simply because we do not know what to do about it! Sometimes, I wondered if God had really bestowed any particular blessing on me by not letting them kill me.

Spiritually, I was clearly walking through prison corridors, blindly bumping into things, (remember I don't see too well in the dark) frustrated at the fact that I could not see any gates of emotional freedom in the distance.

I erroneously felt as if God did not care about children who suffer, but again the Word of God proved me wrong.

Jesus said in Matthew 18:6, "But whoso shall offend one of these little ones which Believe me, it were better for him that a millstone were hanged about his Neck and that he were drowned in the depth of the sea" and in Matthew 18:10, "Take heed that ye despise not one of these little ones; for I say unto you, that in heaven their angels do always behold the face of my Father which is in heaven."

These are just a sampling of the verses I found on God's love for children, and it is enough for me. The message in Matthew 18: 10 is clear: if you harm children, the angels are "telling God on you!"

Until I see God face-to-face, I will not fully understand why I had to suffer, but at least I know now that he is not pleased about my abduction. My kidnapping was an act of someone's selfish wicked heart, and God has allowed us all the right to a free will. We can freely be wicked or freely be good. Most survivors have encountered the wicked.

I finally reasoned that, no matter how much I had suffered, I still needed to keep going and follow and trust God. The apostle Peter became my example. He had suffered, but he followed and trusted anyway.

The story of Peter in prison, found in the book of Acts, was a real catalyst to help my along on my healing journey. I believe that story gives us a road map of healing and I will cover the full story in chapter 5.

Trust is a decision I made, just like any other decision. I was beginning to see that healing is simply a series of decisions firmly made while passing through the prison corridors. Trust is a choice. I chose to trust. I closed my eyes and let Him guide me through the corridors of emotional prison, then the corridors of life. I just closed my eyes.

I cannot keep my eyes wide open to the terrifying things that have not happened. I shut my eyes.

Like Peter's example, I cannot look back into my proverbial prison cell of past pain. I shut my eyes and go forward.

I cannot get myself into a panic attack, worrying that I may bump into a wall, I shut my eyes.

I cannot allow myself to be depressed and listen to misinformed people, telling me that I am too damaged to live well. I can hold on to the garment of Jesus and let him navigate us through the corridors of my life, and I shut my eyes.

At first, it was difficult to rely on God instead of myself, but as weeks, months, and years passed, as I was practicing how to shut my eyes, trust got easier. I slip up every so often and open my eyes, and it always proves to be a mistake. With open eyes, I see all the potential dangerous business in the world and then I am again in an emotional place of despair and hopelessness. I can see the dark side of the mountain coming before me. After experiencing the pain of despair and hopelessness for a while, I remember again to shut my eyes and peace begins again.

When my eyes are open, I am trusting in my vision. When my eyes are closed, I am trusting in God's vision. God's vision is always reliable.

I am learning that no matter how bad my circumstances may be, to shut my eyes and rely on the Lord. My negative circumstances are not the truth of my life, just a temporary annoyance. I shut my eyes and keep going.

Trusting God is the first step of obedience taken if we wish to heal. If the trauma you faced is extensive, this may be a challenge. It was a challenge for me, but I am glad I made the decision because of the healing I enjoy today.

If you do not feel you can trust God, ask him to help you to do so. Ask God to help you close your eyes.

But the salvation of the righteous is of the Lord; He is their strength in time of trouble. And the Lord shall help them and deliver them: he shall deliver them from the wicked, and save them because they trust in him. (Psalm 37:39–40)

Action Plan and Assignment

1. Determine that you will choose to trust God.

2. Add a column to your action plan under the heading of "Trust God." Under this heading, list all the things in your life you wish to give over to God to put in His trust. Some examples might be your children, job, savings, marriage, and many more things too numerous to mention here, but do not forget to give Him your past. When you give Him your past, make sure and list all of the things traumatic events of your past has cost you. Do not worry about making this list too complete or missing something as this will be covered again later. Listing the things that immediately come to your mind will give you a start on concepts to come and a start on your healing.

3. Read all of Psalm 37.

4. Read 1 John 5:3–4.

4

Connect to the Son

It is my firm conviction that true and complete healing cannot come about by psychology and counseling alone, but by the healing touch of the savior Jesus Christ. If we want the healing touch of Jesus, we must make sure that we are "in touch and plugged in" with Jesus.

This is the one more thing to check before we go on to more of the practical applications of healing: we need to make sure that the power source is in place. We need to know that we have the "power" to perform all the upcoming tasks. Our power source is, of course, Jesus Christ himself.

It is entirely possible that as you read this, you are in a state of anger and fighting toward God. Anger toward God is quite common in some cases, but do not let that stop you from reading and doing the action assignments anyway. The anger toward God will be sorted out as you go through the process, and I might add here that the God who created the universe is certainly not going to shrivel up and die because you are mad at him.

Be committed to doing the assignments, reading scripture, and praying anyway. You may not feel like it, but I have learned that when we do the right things, eventually (sometimes immediately) the feelings follow. Do not burden yourself with "feelings" and getting the right "feelings" right now. If we lied about or pretended to have different feelings, God would know anyway. God is more interested in our obedience than he is our feelings.

Think of the feelings as the wagon. Think of doing right, as the horse. The horse pulls the wagon. Doing right pulls the feelings along.

If you are mad at God, it is what it is. Take my advice and move on for now, because I think that the greater capacity to easily get rid of your "God anger" will come in time.

My husband and I own and operate a small ranch. We bought bare ground and built on it piece by piece. Our property is mountainous and very remote. It never occurred to us that it would take tens of thousands of dollars to get electricity! We moved out onto ground so far from civilization that I almost expected dinosaurs to pop out of a time machine and greet me!

My husband, Mark, installed our solar electric power system himself.

Mark started building the house and installed the wiring, but I did not bother to plug in the toaster, since the wiring was not yet connected to the power source. Mark read for three months on the subject of solar power systems; he then purchased the components, built a solar panel array, pointed it to the sun, wired it to the house, and then I could plug in my toaster.

As humans, we need a power source too. Even the addiction organizations like those for alcoholics and other substance abuse support groups agree that if you want the highest success, you need to connect to your higher power. I must warn you now, that if you are serious about healing and living the best life God has for you, you cannot skip this all-important step. The rest of the principles in this book depend on the foundation of "plugging in" to the power source.

Think of it this way, pretend you are a toaster (don't laugh, just follow with me for a bit).

You are a beautiful brand-new toaster. The factory that built you was the best in the world. You are the highest quality and craftsmanship. You have four slots to toast the bread, bagels, and other yummy stuff. You have all the latest mechanisms that make pastries perfect and you even have a buzzer that signals when the food is done.

You are a perfect toaster with just one problem. Unless you are plugged into the power source, all your gleaming beauty and mechanics are worthless. In like fashion, I do not believe you can heal to your highest potential without your power source from Jesus the Christ.

I was not born into a Christian home, so I knew very little of God. My mother told me that there was a God and a Jesus, that I should say prayers before I want to sleep and ask God to make me a good girl, but I knew little else, or maybe I just did not understand any further.

When I was a young teenager, someone invited me to accept Jesus Christ as my savior and power source. I recognized that I was indeed a sinner (even though I tried not to be) and that sinners do not reach heaven. The only way to heaven is to accept the payment of my sin by Jesus when he was crucified.

Anyone reading this who has endured satanic ritual abuse as I have knows that the primary objective for the ritual is to mock Jesus. Hatred of Jesus and God is the driving attitude in devil worship. The things I witnessed and heard about God in these rituals are unspeakable and vile. I will not glorify the devil by repeating them. I will say this though, when someone invited me to have a personal relationship with Jesus, I did not have to give it much thought, because I knew beyond any doubt that there was a devil and demons were real. I had firsthand experience. I witnessed the fact that demons exist, that evil is present, and that death is inevitable.

Jesus was my lifeline. I had had a real taste of hell, now I could learn what heaven was like. Jesus is good, pure, and beautiful. I needed that.

Job 28:28 says, "Behold the fear of the Lord, that is wisdom; and to depart from evil is understanding."

The first step to eternal life and paradise is to fear God and turn away from all evil and wrongdoing. To have a relationship with Jesus, you must repent of your wrongdoing, you must recognize that your sin (wrongdoing) has separated you from a holy God and He is incapable of sin.

Through the years, I have talked to so many survivors that think this truth of repentance does not apply to them. They think that they are exempt because of what they suffered. They think that God will make an exception on their behalf because they suffered so much, and because of their suffering, doing the will of God is too hard.

Many people do think that because they suffered so much, they are incapable of doing much more than suffering. They erroneously think they do not have the power to do right in all circumstances.

I heard a man once say that he would continue to cheat on his wife. He said that God would forgive him anyway (even though his wife was a good wife) because he (God) would take account of the man's circumstances and forgive him anyway. Repentance and right living did not apply to him, or so he thought.

It was obvious that this man never read 1 John 1: 6 which says, "If we say we have fellowship with him, and walk in darkness, we lie, and do not the truth." The atrocities that I suffered were not my fault. God will not hold me accountable for those things. What I will be accountable for are those things that are the words and deeds of my own choosing. Someday, we all will give an account to God for the choices we made. Mankind will not only give an account of our actions, but even our thoughts.

I figured out that if I used my abuse as an excuse to disobey and dishonor God, that I would never completely heal. I knew way back then that I had a choice to do or not to do all the things God asks, I just had to decide how healed I wanted to be. I figured out that, I was not responsible for what I suffered (God would deal with them), but I was responsible for how I reacted to it.

I have made a note to myself in my Bible at Job 38. This is where God speaks and Job is listening to God. The note I wrote to myself says, "Job stops listening to friends and listens to God—the beginning of healing." When you read the whole book of Job, I know you will agree that his healing *did* start when he started listening to God.

In the book of Job, we learn of the intense suffering of Job. His children all die, his worldly possessions are gone, and his body is in pain with boils and disease. In the midst of his suffering, He listens to God. Job embraces God's words with his whole heart and soul. Job accepts everything God has to say, even the things that are difficult to hear. Job sees that he is a sinner. God then speaks from chapter 38 to 41. Then Job speaks in chapter 42:1–2 and 6, "Then Job answered the Lord, and said I know that thou can do everything and that no thought can be withheld from thee, Wherefore I abhor myself and repent."

Why is this the beginning of healing? you ask. Because to begin to heal, we must see ourselves for who we are, just like Job did.

People who have been victimized and traumatized can get stuck here.

The truth is that no matter what we have suffered and endured, we still have to accept the truth that we are sinners. Trauma does not change or negate that as the book of Job illustrates.

None of us could ever be good enough to please a Holy God and creator, so because he loves us in spite of our sin, He provided a way for us to be blessed and healed. The way is Jesus the Christ.

> But God commended his love towards us in that while we were yet sinners, Christ died for us. Much more then, being now justified by his blood we shall be saved from wrath through him. (Romans 5:8–9)

For the wages of sin is death, but the gift of God is eternal life through Jesus Christ our Lord. (Romans 6:23)

To activate, or plug into my power source:

If thou shall confess with thy mouth the Lord Jesus, and shalt believe in thine heart that God hath raised him from the dead, thou shalt be saved. For with the heart man believeth unto righteousness; and with the mouth confession is made unto salvation. (Romans 10:9–10)

Notice here that there are just two things needed for eternal life and healing:

1.   Repentance, to realize that you have wronged a holy God.
     Again I say, do not get trapped by the devil here and let him tell you that others have wronged you more, so this does not apply to you. God will judge those who have hurt you. They have to answer to him on their own, and they will be accountable. Just be concerned with yourself right now and trust Him.
     As you progress in your healing, there may be other times when you think that the subject does not belong to you because you were damaged so much. Sometimes, I had to remind myself repeatedly that obedience to God is not conditional. I cannot use my past as an excuse, and if I do, the misery will be mine, not because God is punishing me, but because I am living in the past and I am punishing myself.
     Obedience to God by accepting Jesus as the payment for our sins is the "get out of jail card" that promotes our healing.
     What happened to me was vile, but what actions and thoughts I did on my own after that were of my own choosing. Some actions of mine may have been influenced by my abduction, but I still chose to do them.

So forget about what happened to you for just a short while, at least long enough to focus on what you need to do to plug into your power source, and that first step is to confess that you are not right with God and accept that with His death, Jesus made payment of your sin. He took the punishment that we all deserve. If we accept his death and resurrection as payment for our sins, we get plugged in.

2. Accept that with His death, Jesus made payment of your sin. He took the punishment that we all deserve. If we accept his death and resurrection as payment for our sins, we get plugged in.

If you have never done this before, you are now taking the first steps on the most amazing adventure of your life!

After accepting Christ and going through the process of healing, I can now say that I am almost glad that those awful people abducted me. I have come to that point because of my walk with God, and that walk would not have been as close if I had not suffered so much.

This attitude did not happen right away, but came about through a process of walking through the corridors of the emotional prison with Christ, step by step. I now know that I personally would never have had such a close walk with Jesus, had I not suffered. I am blessed far more than I probably would have been. The biblical Peter who is our example, who later wrote the book of first Peter, tells us the same thing about suffering.

> Forasmuch then as Christ hath suffered in the flesh, arm yourselves with the same mind: for he that hath suffered in the flesh hath ceased from sin; That he no longer should live the rest of his time in the flesh to the lusts of men, but to the will of God. (1 Peter 4:1–2)

You are probably not ready at this point yet to embrace the concept of "suffering can be a good thing," and that is perfectly fine.

If you have truly plugged into your power source by accepting the Lord Jesus as you personal savior for your sins, Psalm 91:14–15 is just for you ! God is speaking when he says:

> Because he hath set his love upon me, therefore will I deliver him: I will set him on high, because he hath known my name. He shall call upon me and I will answer him: I will be with him in trouble; I Will deliver him, and honor him. (Psalm 91:14–15)

Notice here that God did not promise that I would not have trouble, but he did promise that if I set my love upon Him, he would deliver me. Healing is deliverance.

My journey has not been without additional sorrows and mistakes that I made, but the power source I have in Jesus keeps me going, brings me joy, offers me strength, gives me comfort, and has healed my pain.

The word of God tells us to make your calling and election sure; in other words, be very sure that you have plugged into the power.

I have traveled in my car quite a lot. In 1996, I put 35,000 miles on my car all by myself. Some subsequent years have watched me drive almost as much. I have always been a bit nervous of breakdowns, so I have made myself a mechanical student.

I found that a good auto mechanic is like a good computer geek. They love to talk about their craft.

Show a mechanic that you are a willing pupil, and he will teach you all you want to know. I have been a willing pupil. I have listened and learned carefully.

Driving down the road, I can make a pretty good diagnosis as to what may be wrong with my car. Lights dimming: alternator, knocking noise when I turn: U joint, and so on. I can tell when the shocks are wearing, a tire needs attention, and all sorts of things that may impress the average person.

I have lots of knowledge, but I cannot fix my car. I could not identify the parts, nor would I know how to install them. I am not a mechanic. I have some understanding about mechanics, but I am not a mechanic. My relationship with my car is not that intimate.

Make sure that you do not just have an understanding of God, but a real relationship. Make sure that you fully understand that it was the blood of Jesus that paid the price for your sins, past, present, and future. Love him for that and embrace him.

I know from my ritual abuse that the devil has much understanding of God, but he is not surrendered and he does not love Him.

Action Assignment

1. Read the book of Job, especially chapters 38 to 42. 2. For comfort, read Psalm 34.

2. Pray and ask God to forgive your sin and make Jesus the Lord and comfort of your life and to heal you.

3. Read Hebrews 7: 25.

4. Read Luke 13: 5.

The predominant attitude in the world now is; we cannot hold the person (rapist, murderer, thief, etc) too responsible because they had a bad childhood or a traumatic experience. I have read the Bible cover to cover and can safely say, the Word of God does not support that erroneous thinking.

5

Peter Is in Prison

Acts 12 tells us of one account of Peter put into prison. King Herod had killed James, the brother of John, and then had Peter arrested and put him into prison. With many soldiers standing guard, Herod was certain that Peter could not escape. The Bible tells us that Peter was sleeping between two soldiers, bound with chains, and the keepers of the door kept the prison (12:6). Peter is in a pretty tough spot. Multiple men are ensuring that he will not escape.

We then see in verse 7 that the angel of the Lord came upon him, and a light shone in the prison and he (the angel) hit Peter on the side and made him to get up by saying, "Arise up quickly." The chains then fell from Peter's hands.

In verse 8, the angel said unto him, "Gird thyself and bind on thy sandals," and so he did. And he says to him, "Cast thy garment about thee and follow me."

In verse 9, we see that Peter went out and followed him, and in verse 10 when they were past the first and second ward, they came to the iron gate that leads to the city, which opened of its own accord, and they went out through one street and the angel departed from him. This is one of my favorite stories from the Bible. The story shows us the power of prayer, of course (Peter's friends had been praying for him to be released), but there is so much more to learn from this passage of scripture.

Whenever I feel like whining about anything, I try to think of Peter in prison.

Whether you are just starting your healing adventure or have been on this path for a while, the true account of Peter in prison is a part of scripture you should refer back to, often, to inspire you.

Let's look at the story more closely. Peter is bound tightly with chains and at least four guards are around him. Two soldiers were at his side and probably two more were at the door. I think it is interesting to note here that, while Peter's prospects are pretty bleak, he was sleeping. I think most people would be wide awake and profusely sweating with worry. Not Peter, he was resting without even a tranquilizer pill!

So in looking at the events a little more closely, we see that when the angel comes into the cell and wakes Peter from his sleep, then the angel says something very interesting, he tells Peter to get up.

When Peter gets up, the chains fall off. Just a simple act of obedience on Peter's part caused chains of bondage to fall off. The guards did not even wake up with all those chains rattling.

Notice here that the angel does not pull Peter onto his feet. Peter is capable of standing.

Notice that the chains fall off because Peter cannot do that for himself, God does that for him.

Next, the angel tells him to put on his shoes, and Peter obeys. Peter does not tell the angel that his prospects are impossible. He does not command the angel to look at the guards and admit that this behavior is too dangerous; what if they wake up and catch him! Peter does not give the angel a teary monologue of his awful plight and ask for his pity.

Peter does not whine or complain about having to lace his own sandals, even though the ordeal of being humiliated and mistreated by these people was a lot to bear for any human. Peter does not give arguments and excuses, he just obeys.

I am sure the angel could have tied on the sandals for him, but he does not because Peter can do that for himself. Even if his wrists were sore from the shackles, Peter was capable.

After the shoes are secure, the angel tells Peter to put his coat on. Again, Peter obeys without question, and the angel does not say, "Here, Peter, let me help you." Why would the angel need to assist? Peter can put on his own coat, regardless of his circumstances.

The angel gives Peter another order: "Follow me," he says, and Peter again obeys. Peter does not ask the angel to carry him through the prison because Peter can walk by himself.

Peter and the angel go right past all the soldiers. The guards could have been asleep or temporarily blinded, I do not know, but whatever happened came about by God. The pair walked through all of the dark dingy corridors, and we know it would have been impossible to just walk by so many men, unless God did it for him.

When the pair came to the iron gates, God opens the gates because Peter cannot do that for himself either.

Notice in each instance, *all* the things that Peter is capable of doing, he is expected to perform. After being jailed, he was probably sore, maybe bruised, maybe even a little weak from hunger, but he did the things he was told to do because, in spite of his uncomfortable circumstances, he could do the tasks.

It is to be noted here that we sometimes are comfortable and content to whine and give excuses as to why we cannot heal or do even simple things God asks, instead of obeying the voice of the Lord and watching him open the iron gates of our lives. It cannot be overstated here that all the things we are incapable of doing (even in relation to healing) will be done by our Creator, and all the things we *are* capable of doing, He will expect us to do.

You might be feeling like you are in prison now. The pain, loss, sorrow, and humiliation you feel are in themselves a prison. You may be in an emotional prison, bound with chains of anger and despair. Your prison is every bit as real as the bricks and mortar prison that Peter was in.

God wants to lead you out of your emotional prison as well. He will take you through the dark corridors to the gates and can always be relied upon to do what you cannot do for yourself. There might be spots along the way that you might be unwilling to do. This happens to us all, but He will wait for you. Stop at that point and work with the Lord till you are ready to perform the task, then go to the next thing. You do not want to stay at one point and never completely heal, do you?

I mentioned earlier, the personal trainer, who told me that I did not have to do all the stuff she told me, I just had to decide how fat I wanted to be? The same applies here. You do not have to do all God tells you to do; you just have to decide how much you want to heal. I made the decision that I did not want to wander in dark, bleak, emotional corridors for the rest of my life. I made some decisions to do some difficult things, but they were worth it.

One afternoon, many years ago, I was sitting in group therapy, listening to all the other women talk. I had only been going to the group a short while, and I found it helpful to hear others, knowing that I was not alone in my feelings and hurts. At first, I found it soothing to be in a group of other ladies who had also suffered some kind of trauma.

On this particular day, I became curious as to how long these ladies had been in therapy. I was new to the therapeutic party and was anxious for the pain to stop and the good feelings to be the norm of my life.

I asked if each lady could tell me how long she had been in therapy, working on her healing. I wanted to get a rough idea of how long it would be till I began to feel all warm and fuzzy inside.

Their answers gave me great distress. The average woman had been in therapy for about fifteen years and had not progressed in her healing any more than I had done in a few months!

I was depressed all the rest of the day. I did not want to hurt for the rest of my life! I did not want to walk through dark emotional corridors for even fifteen years! I wanted to heal. I wanted my trauma to be scars only, not seeping sores! I wanted to feel better. I wanted to live an abundant life!

If Jesus is our healer like the Bible says, then there had to be a way to escape the prison corridors. But how could I? All of these ladies were Christians and they had not found the way.

What was wrong?

I stopped attending the group because these questions bothered me too much. I searched the scriptures more carefully and found Peter in prison. I knew from the text that I would be required to do some things in relation to my emotional healing, but I didn't know what. At this point, I was willing to do anything! I just did not want to hurt anymore! I asked God to show me the way.

The answer to my prayer was actually very simple. God wants me out of emotional prison. God will do for me what I cannot do and I am expected to do what I can. If I am obedient, one day, the iron gates will fly open and I will be free. I am happy to report that the iron gates have indeed come open for me, and although I have scars, we all know that scars are not so painful, they are just a reminder of what we went through.

At first, these ideas of obedience angered me. What was inflicted on me was not *my* fault! Why should I be expected to work at this when no sin of mine caused this pain? Why can't God just wave his magic wand and make all the hurts and consequences go away magically? That is, of course, after he thoroughly punishes all those people who hurt me! And it would be very kind of him to let me watch them getting what they deserved!

I think this is the point that most victims stay at. Most of the people that I have talked to who have been victimized; do not get beyond this point. They find it impossible to get beyond the feelings of indignation and wrath. After all, when we have been treated unfairly, we think we have the right to not only stay angry, but demand that "someone" do something about it.

I think that Peter could have given these same arguments. He could have indignantly showed the angel his wounds and demanded to have a tantrum first. He had a right to be angry! He was put in prison on totally false pretenses! He could have shown the angel his bruises and demanded that the guards be punished first, then he would follow! Peter could have told the angel how sore he was from the beatings and asked for assistance in putting on his shoes. Maybe he would have liked the angel to carry him through the prison, or better yet, just wave his magic wand and the pair would instantly be out. After all, walking takes effort when you are sore!

I gave these concepts an incredible amount of thought. All therapists I visited encouraged me to "get it all out." I did this without argument, but I decided I wanted more in my life than to just go over and relive the abuse every therapy session. It seemed to me that as long as I kept repeating the details over and over, I was stuck in neutral.

Do not misunderstand me here: it is important to go over the acts of humiliation and violence you suffered, preferably with a good qualified therapist, but there comes a time if you want to heal, you have to move on. Repeating the details once a week for years did not appear to be working for anyone else, so I chose another path.

One day, I felt as if I had related the injustices I had suffered enough times. I did not want to be a victim all my life. I wanted to be a survivor. It was time to move on, to put on my sandals and coat and follow the angel through to the gates...but how?

The healing concepts are actually quite simple, but the work can be difficult at times, simply because retraining the brain requires a lot of work. It took a conscious effort on my part to rethink, readjust, and live well. I am sorry to have to tell you that sometimes the difficulty seemed overwhelming, but the amazing results I enjoy were well worth the effort!

When I first began my adventure in healing, I still had thoughts that the tasks were unfair. This sometimes made me a bit unwilling to do the work necessary to heal and I would slip back into the initial feelings of anger and self-loathing as if the abduction happened that day. This is a dark spot to be in and no one should want to live in a dark place.

To counteract the dark spots, I developed an attitude that helped me not only to get through the dark place, but to go on to take all the other necessary steps to heal completely. My strategy was simple. I knew that the agenda of these people (powered by Satan himself) was to destroy not only my life, but the lives of all the people that I loved. Those who hurt me were wicked and selfish people that wanted me to hurt beyond the abuse they inflicted upon me. I figured out that if I stayed in an emotional crippling place (like anger), they won. They achieved their goal! They could ruin my life, take almost total control of me, and keep me from the healing gates, even though I never saw them again.

Satan's plan is the same for everyone who has suffered trauma. His plan is to keep us chained to the guards in the middle of our emotional prison.

I reasoned that, if I did not figure a way to get beyond all of this, that these evil people were in a way, doing their evil to me over and over again until I took control. As long as I was reliving the past, the past would define my life as well as define me. I found this unacceptable.

Remembering the past is not the same as reliving it. As long as my pain remained, I was reliving the past.

My next step was an attitude overhaul. I decided that I would stop thinking and acting like a victim and start acting like a victorious warrior. This you can do also.

You may be thinking that you cannot achieve this warrior thinking because you do not know how. The first step in learning how to be a warrior is just a bit of self-affirming talk.

It is simple. Tell yourself that you are a survivor, and you are overcoming. It matters not that you do not "feel" like a survivor, what matters is that you look in the mirror every day and tell yourself you are till it feels right.

Yes, I know this can be difficult, and as a member of the "I survived trauma" club, I think I can comment, but if you do not make a conscious decision to change your attitude, evil wins. You do not want those that caused you such pain to win, do you? You may have had a tough start in the race of life, but no one focuses on the start of the race because the glory is at the finish line.

This is your life, choose to take control.

Self-affirming talk is biblical.

In Ezekiel 37:1–14 is the account of God talking to the prophet and God tells him something very interesting. God tells the prophet to use his voice to talk to dry bones. I know that the primary meaning of this text is God telling the children of Israel that He will someday restore them, but I think that we all can learn something else here also. When Ezekiel talked to the dry bones, which of course are dead people, he said, "Thus says the Lord God unto these bones; Behold I will cause breath to enter into you and you shall live."

The Bible tells us that the bones did indeed grow muscle and tendons and came to life.

When I first read this account for myself, the message was clear: our words are powerful! We need to say affirmative things to ourselves to counteract the negative prophecies that others have spoken into our lives.

If you think this has no merit, then let me challenge you to think about the parent that continually tells his child that he/she is stupid. Modern psychology has proven that that people who have such negative words constantly spoken over them usually will act stupid, even if they are highly intelligent.

Our words are powerful and we must speak the positive into our lives, even if we do not feel or believe them. The feelings and beliefs will come.

What happened to you is dry bones. Speak life into your dry bones and begin to live. I needed to tell myself that I would be well, that I would finish with victory. I needed to tell myself (out loud, if necessary) that all the things they spoke over me in the ritual were nothing but garbage and had no truth to them.

I needed to tell myself that I was reclaiming my identity (though at that time I did not know what it was) and I would put on my shoes and walk through to the gates of freedom.

I will say again that you may not stop feeling like a victim instantly. Consciously stop thinking like a victim and prophesy good things into your life. You need to change your mind and that takes real effort as well as time. Here I suggest working with a therapist on this if you can. As you talk over your daily feelings and reactions to the therapist, a good counselor will point out when you are engaging in victim mentality and will help you do something new. In other words, the therapist you choose should help you recognize the faulty thinking you repeat and help you to write a new script to go by if the situation should happen again.

If the counselor you are seeing does not offer helpful suggestions, but only listens, nods, and makes notes, you may want to fire him. I fired a few before I found people who would interact with me to get me thinking and acting in the right direction. You need to take charge of your healing. Do not trust someone to do a good job with this just because their credentials are good or is the pastor of a church. They may have impressive credentials and/ or be a wonderful preacher, but this person may not be the right fit for you. Hire someone that is as excited about your efforts as you are. This is your life, take control!

I cannot emphasize enough of what I have already stated, that is real work. There may be days when you need to remind yourself multiple times to put on a warrior attitude and dump the victim thinking. Put up notes in your house and car if you have to. Recite verses of scripture that give you comfort. Stop associations with people who do not support your effort to heal.

Just keep speaking life into the dry bones.

I can promise you that if you will work on this change of mind-set, that it will become easier and easier. As you reboot your system, you will not be fighting the victim mentality as often. Put the next steps of healing into production in your life, coupled with a warrior mentality, and one day, you may find that you are not fighting the victim mentality at all anymore.

Remember that when Peter was in prison, God sent an angel to help him along the way. They worked together, Peter and the angel, to achieve the victory. The Word of God teaches us that angels walk among us, and even the apostle Paul stated that "some have entertained angels unawares." How the Lord sends angels or people and circumstances for healing will be different in everyone's life. You just need to trust that they will be in place as you do you work.

Some days did not go so well for me. Those were the times that I refused to "put on my shoes" or "put on my garment" myself. I now know that my healing was always my decision, and when I made the right decision in a proper attitude, God did the rest for me.

Sometimes, I chose to have a "pity and gripe session" that slowed down my walk to the iron gates of freedom. At those times, I was the lead writer, actor, and even the audience in my drama. I am so grateful that when I chose these negative paths, that God patiently waited for me to "put on my shoes" and walk again. He was there, just waiting for me to stop my childish tantrum, so he could help me get on with the business of getting out of emotional jail. You might experience times like that, where you slip back into the dark places where you can only see the chains and prison walls. Do not worry, He will wait for you.

Again, you might be asking yourself why you should be making any effort at all when the events that took place were not your choice, but brought upon you. It does not seem fair, but do not allow yourself to get stuck in the "fairness cycle." Focus on getting out of prison. Believe that God is with you as you go through the corridors, and move closer and closer to the iron gates. If you keep the course, chances are that one day those gates will open for you and you will be free. Listen and obey like Peter did and stand up! A warrior does not face the enemy being comfortably relaxed!

Action Assignment

1. Read Ezekiel 37:1–18. Think about or discuss how our words are powerful prophecies.

2. Read Acts 12. Think about or discuss the true story about Peter being in prison, and think about how those simple acts of obedience caused chains of bondage to fall off. Emotional pain can be chains of bondage; ask God to show you today what simple act of obedience you can do to cause some of your emotional chins of bondage to disappear.

3. Do affirmative self-talk today.

4. Remember that no one should focus on the start of the race because the glory is at the finish line.

5. Determine to obey God. Read 1 Samuel 15:22–23.

6. To obey is better than sacrifice, and it is the "get out of jail card" that my healing needs.

7. Read Joshua 2:1. This passage of scripture also shows that although God has assured the victory, there are still things for us to do. God will do for you what you cannot do for yourself, He expects you to do the things you can do for yourself.

8. Read Psalm 142:7.

Rehearsing the pain over and over again never healed anyone.

6

Jesus, the Ultimate Therapist

No writing about healing would be complete without a talk on choosing the best therapist you can. I have saved this bit of advice till now, because sometimes it is helpful to choose someone or get into a group therapy and then make a final choice as to your therapist. That is, if you feel you need one. If your hurt and pain is manageable without someone's help and intervention, that is fine, but some of us need a bit more help. After a bit of experience, you can make a more informed decision.

The average self-help book on the subject of trauma and loss has no word on the advice I give now. It was my experience that the general therapeutic community of PhDs, therapists, counselors, pastors, and similar helpers, for the most part, do not seem to fully understand what I will speak to you about now simply because they probably have not had my trauma and experiences. Some things are not learned in textbooks the way that life can teach us. Therapists are like any other professional people in that there are very skilled ones, and then there are a few that are really not too helpful. You must decide who is doing you the most good and above all, who you feel comfortable with. If you are the least bit uncomfortable, maybe it is time to shop for a new counselor. Remember, they work for you. It is not your job to make them feel good about themselves, it is their job to give you the tools you need to heal and have a more successful life.

Initially, it felt good to finally tell the awful truth to someone, but after the telling, I needed to move on. For me, it was not helpful to just talk to someone and for that someone just to take notes and nod his head. Simply telling the trauma again and again did not help me heal to the point I wanted. I needed someone skilled enough to give me the tools to move on, not just relive the same story week after week. I seemed to be stuck in the same place and that place was still a victim mentality. I did not want to live the rest of my life here. I had been a victim too long already.

I tried several preachers, but although I truly believe they were sincere and doing their best, the ones I counseled with were skipping important parts of my healing. As I counseled with pastors, they thought I should go from the telling of the trauma to directly forgiving the evil people.

Forgiveness is part of healing, but omitting critical steps needed for the preparation of forgiveness left me frustrated and feeling guilty. Why couldn't I just forgive and forget? It certainly would make things easier.

What they were counseling me to do was impossible, but trying to tell them otherwise earned me lectures on how wicked and disobedient to God I was, and there was no other way for me to feel better.

A few of them were adamant that all I needed to do was to do good, and I would feel better, be happy, and all would be well. Their advice was that a person did not even need to talk about the trauma; in fact, a person should ignore the past all together. Just do things like getting involved in church work and everything would be perfect! I really hoped that this tactic would work, but as this was the way I had been living my life since salvation and I still did not feel okay, I decided that this was not the best way. I had been trying to do my best all my life, sometimes going beyond what was required of me, and I still felt bad. I still struggled. I still felt like a victim, and I was still angry with the people who abducted me. I decided that there must be something wrong with me.

I thought that I must be really wicked and really evil to not be able to forgive yet. I must be the scum of the earth to not be able to just do good and get over the past. I decided that I must be damaged. My self-esteem was at an all-time low. Counseling someone to forgive before they have thoroughly processed their feelings can be very damaging to the victim. A proper process of the emotions prepares and empowers the person to be able to forgive.

I contacted a few more conventional therapists who, after a few sessions, told me that the kind of trauma I experienced was not covered in any of their textbooks and they could not help me. Maybe I was too damaged. I contemplated suicide. After all, anyone as damaged as I was could not be good for anything, if no one could help me.

I know now that the intentions of all my would-be counselors were good, and they were doing their best, but after a few weeks of sessions, I surmised that the people that I was counseling with might not know that to properly find the iron gates like Peter did. I would need to walk through those corridors. I needed to go through the proper channels and steps. Skipping steps would only frustrate and prolong my suffering.

I am not criticizing the people who tried to help me. Again, I will say that I think they were doing their best, but they were trying to help me from things they learned in books and materials that were written by people who have never traveled this path I was on. I could compare this to, say, teaching someone to swim by pushing them off the dock because the "teacher" had never been swimming.

Omitting some steps in the healing process is like baking a cake and deleting the sugar and leavening, then being upset because the cake did not turn out. Intentions were good, but nothing really turns out well with only good intentions. We need a plan, actions, and information pertinent to the problem. Good intentions are the beginning way to fix the problem, but not the complete solution. God does not overlook the rules of the universe because someone's intentions were good. These good-intentioned people did not understand that I needed a plan.

A building contractor would never dream of building a house without a well-laid-out and accurate plan. We need a plan to if we are to heal in the shortest amount of time and live our best life. I formulated my action plan, the same one I share with you.

In other words, I figured out that if I go against some natural order, the natural order may bite me in the behind. I had to figure it out because I wanted to live a normal happy life. All things must be done decently and in order and your healing is no exception.

God could have transported Peter from the prison cell to the outside in a twinkling, but He did not. I believe that God did not immediately transform Peter from the cell to the outdoors, so we all could learn some important things. Most things in life are a process. If you want a college education, you do not just go in and get you diploma. It is a process that you work at. Babies are not conceived one day then born the next. The seasons change through a process, buildings are created through a process, airline trips start at the ticket counter, and most things worthwhile involve a proper process.

Unfortunately, sometimes, I found the healing process to be as painful as surgery, but I can say that the result is well worth the pain!

After much prayer, God did guide me to the right people to counsel me. I found a few Christian therapists who were invaluable in my progression through the corridors of my emotional prison to freedom. I am grateful to them and grateful to God for providing them.

For me, people with PHDs were more helpful than regular counselors. They seemed to be more skilled in helping me sort out my past and move on. Again, remember that my trauma was unusually severe. Yours may be not as complicated and a church counselor, mental health advisor, or preacher would do nicely.

God has just the person to help you, pray and ask Him to give you your best choice.

You could be blessed in that the preacher of your church has a God-given talent to help you through the corridors. A man of God skilled in the Word and in psychology! Use your judgment and find your best option.

The point of this message is to help you choose someone who can work well with you. If you follow the action plans carefully, it is possible to do all on your own or even work with a friend who cares enough to take the time. If your trauma is as severe as mine was, I strongly suggest that you work with a licensed therapist. Ask God to guide you to just the right person.

I asked God to help me write this book in way that, if you cannot find a person to work with, or cannot afford one, the assignments in this book can act as a helper. You can heal on your own without help, but I think it is easier and maybe even faster if you have someone to "bounce your thoughts off of."

I think that Exodus 17:10–16 was written just to cover this subject. Moses needed some help from his friends to assure that the Israelites gained a victory. We need help sometimes too.

It was embarrassing for me to initially seek out help. The stigma of the whole process was troubling to me. You may feel the same way, but let me encourage you to get past it.

Some people close to you may mock or accuse you. That was one of my problems. A family member mocked and accused me of "being crazy." This person snuck into my bedroom and went through my personal journals where I was trying to write out my feelings and experiences. I was not ready to allow others access to this information yet, so the experience was very disturbing.

Then, this person spread vicious rumors about me, saying that I was dangerous to the safety of others simply because I had the courage to seek professional help.

I include this experience because I have talked to so many survivors who have had similar problems. What kind of person can be so mean and judgmental to another human being who has suffered so much? This kind of person has no compassion for others and that truly is a shame. What kind of person kicks you when you are already so damaged and hurting? This is a kind of person you should avoid. It matters little if the person is family, coworker, or anyone else, this person is not helpful to your healing. It is possible that someday this kind of person could see the error of her/his behavior and your relationship could be restored, but for now, do what is best for you. Negative attitudes cause more hurt and you have enough hurt to deal with now. Limit time with anyone who is unsupportive.

Be good to yourself and allow yourself the time and attention you need to heal.

Action Plan and Assignment

1. Ask God to bring you some wonderful people into your life to provide encouragement, support, and help for your healing.

2. Read Exodus 17:10–16.

3. Read James 1: 5.

4. Remember that the best therapist you can find is Jesus. Jesus has experienced every humiliation and pain that you have experienced. Jesus gets it, He understands, therefore, He has the answers to get you healed and victorious, do not neglect to get into the Word of God every day, where all the answers to life are. God will speak to you.

5. Read Luke 14:28–32 and think about the fact that everyone needs a plan.

6. Remember Peter in prison, God was his ultimate rescuer.

7. Read Philippians 2:9–11 and 3:10.

> O sing unto the Lord a new song; for He hath done marvelous things. (Psalm 98:1)

7

Manage Grief, Loss, and Triggers

Any psychologist or therapist worth a nickel will tell you that to heal, you must go through a period of grieving the things you have lost. It matters little what kind of trauma you have suffered when it comes to grief and loss because when you have trauma, you have suffered loss.

I lost my childhood. Perhaps you did too as well. Perhaps you will never have children because of what you have suffered. Perhaps you have lost a family because of their non-support of you in your distress. You may have lost income, dignity, self-esteem, a spouse, or even your health because of someone else's act of selfish wickedness.

I suffer mild seizures that are a direct result of repeated beatings to my head. Not enjoying complete health is certainly a reason to grieve the loss of a healthy body.

The things you have lost need to be identified and grieved. I suggest you make a list or keep a journal for a while to get in touch with these feelings of loss.

If you do not realize fully what you have lost, your subconscious mind will remind you daily or hourly and you will have a more difficult time coping with trigger emotions and no effective way to deal with them.

Certain pictures, places, phrases, things, colors, situations, people, and other images remind you of your trauma. If you feel physical and emotional discomfort when certain situations arise, we call these things "triggers." When these "triggers" occur in your life, you experience the trauma all over again, with all the emotional pain, physical pain, and fear. These are flashbacks of the worst sort because you are living in every way the horror all over again as if it happened just at that moment.

People who have never experienced trauma will not understand the concept of triggers. You can try to explain it to them, however, so that if you are triggered in their presence, they will have a better understanding.

Being "triggered" by a person, place, or thing, is common for anyone suffering from post–traumatic stress disorder. Only a qualified therapist or psychologist can diagnose post–traumatic stress disorder (PTSD), but whether you have the disorder or not (and most of us who have suffered trauma do), you can still experience triggers that cause you to be emotionally right back in that place of abuse and pain.

To identify the things you have lost and grieve them are the first steps in disarming the triggers that plague your life.

Going through this identification process with a qualified therapist may help you. This can be done by yourself, but sometimes, the amount of loss you suffer will only be evident with someone outside yourself and family.

Go to your counseling session ready with a pen and paper, and as you realize a point of loss (let's use childhood as an example), write it down. Under the heading of "childhood," you will put down all the things that a normal child experiences that you did not experience. These are your losses. Be as complete as you can so that you can disarm the triggers as best as you can. For example, going to bed without fear and apprehension is normal for a "normal" child. If you are survivor of childhood rape or incest, you have not had that luxury. Do not think it trivial or silly to list something like "peaceful fearless sleep." Fearless and peaceful sleep must be a wonderful thing. I was only five years old, so I do not really remember what it was like to "feel safe" and secure when I went to bed each night. This was taken from me. This is one of the many losses that I had to grieve.

Do not let your list of losses overwhelm you. Your list may be quite lengthy, maybe even a page or more, but most people will not have such an extensive list. Do not allow yourself to feel that this is an impossible task. It is not an impossible task, just take one thing at a time. Some things you may be able to grieve quickly and easily and some will take more time. Be patient with yourself.

Still using the bedtime safety and fear example, the good news is that I cope well. I cope with prayer at bedtime and trust in God that he will protect me and keep me safe. I also am careful about which books or TV programs I watch before my head connects with the pillow. Many people like all the action-packed shoot-'em-up movies. It seems to me that these movies most often have stuff being blown up or images of children or women being hurt. Why do screenwriters think that women being raped make good TV? This kind of story does not affect people who have never experienced these things firsthand. For them, this is just a story, but for the rest of us, this storyline and violence could be a trigger.

These kinds of images will ensure that I will not sleep well and have repeated nightmares. If I have eaten anything before I went to bed, the experience is intensified. There are many other things I can list under loss of childhood. Each point must be looked at, cried over, felt the loss, and then moved on.

None of us is Superman. We do not leap tall buildings in a single bound; neither can we deal with every aspect other the traumatic losses we have suffered all at once. Break it down into an action plan.

Action Plan is as follows:

1. Make your grief list.

2. Grieve each point.

3. Set a time limit to grieve.

4. Highlight the losses that are not permanent.

It may seem cruel to say to someone that you must limit the grief period, but believe me, grief for the rest of your life is the real cruelty. Choosing to stop the grief process is an act of the will. It is something you do deliberately after you have done your anger and grief work. You need to *choose* to move on At this point, you may think that this is impossible and the words "I can't" might be easily formed in your thoughts, so let's make it more manageable and easier.

Take your action plan in hand and looking over your lists, break each point down into more specific workable points. Be sad for each point, one at a time, and this can make the process more manageable and bearable. Note here that this may take days, weeks, months, or even years, depending on your degree of pain and how quickly you choose to look at each point of loss.

For instance, one of your grief points might be a loss of dignity. Under loss of dignity, you might list the inability to speak in public, extreme shyness, loss of self-esteem, and opportunities lost as a result of any of these attitudes. There are many other losses to be listed under dignity, but I mentioned these because these particular things could have been lost in the past, but now you can regain them. These are the things on your list that you need to highlight in yellow pen. These are the things that maybe were a direct result of your trauma, but do not need to be a part of your life script anymore.

The past is gone. You cannot change what transpired then, but you can change your thinking and behaviors now. You can change those behaviors and thinking that has been a part of you, and now you choose never to think and feel that way again. Past traumas do not have to directly affect you all of your life. There are many things you can change and then go on to live a full and happy life. If I am not making myself too clear for some of you, please let me be redundant and put it this way: your action plan helps you to see many aspects of your grief and personality that you may not have thought of before. If you are a shy person, you may not have realized that your shyness was a direct result of your trauma, but it might be. Poor self-esteem, self-hatred, depression, timidity, fearfulness, perfectionism, and many personality traits might be a direct result of the hurt and pain you have suffered. This is where you might need a qualified therapist to help you.

Some personality traits you might choose to keep, even though they were results of your pain, but who wants to keep low self-esteem or self-hatred?

I cannot emphasize enough to look at each loss and each aspect of loss carefully and one at a time. Focus on that particular loss. Cry and experience the sadness, then tell yourself that you have been sad long enough and are ready to move on.

Come up with a workable solution to deal with every loss. Your coping solution might be medication. There is no shame in taking medication if you need to. No one makes a diabetic feel shame when he needs an insulin injection. Talk to your doctor. Tell your doctor of your trauma and ask if medication could help you. Your doctor should be a good judge of the benefits and risks of medication.

As you work through your action plan, take another color of highlighter pen and highlight the triggers. Identify and list all of the possible triggers that could possibly make you feel that loss again. Once you have decided to move on, you do not want to be triggered into reliving it again!

List workable solutions to avoid the triggers in the future. This one actually can be fun! Make the solutions as pleasant for yourself as possible. For example, if a certain place triggers you, your solution could be going somewhere enjoyable and fun instead of visiting a dark place!

When you feel you have done a thorough job of exercising control over a certain point, move on to the next point. Go as fast or slow as you need, but march right down your list.

If you get triggered again over a certain point, refer back to the solution you wrote down. I know it sounds silly to do all this writing, but you will be surprised at how often you come up with a solution, get triggered, and then forget what you had decided to do about it.

If your trigger happens to be a person, limit or completely eliminate that person from your life. If the trigger is a place or type of place, avoid it. If any behavior of your own brings on a trigger, change your behavior.

Part of satanic ritual abuse is being locked in a coffin. Any small claustrophobic space can trigger a negative experience in me. Tiny bathrooms, elevators, congested rooms, and even caves used to bring on an immediate panic response in me. I am pleased to say that I cope really well now in these situations and can be in these places now and rarely have a panic thought! Getting to this point took some work. Getting your mind to practice a different response to fear works well in some situations.

All the people that tortured, bled, and ritualized me are dead, but if I were to see them face-to-face today, it would be difficult, if not impossible, for me to keep my composure. Be realistic in the things you can achieve and be realistic about the things you cannot change. A certain person may trigger you, but your chances of changing that person are zero. You can only control you, not others.

In other words, do your best, but do not be too hard on yourself. Do not allow yourself to be stuck in a particular grief point. You need to allow the grief, then move on, and you may need your therapist to help you with this. Do not feel guilty if you need behavior modifications to help you move on. Some examples of behavior modifications would be avoiding certain books, movies, people, places and things that upset you. In time, some of these may be added back when you have achieved a certain level of victory over them, and some things you may choose to never let back into your life.

I have a personal list of things that do not trigger me anymore, but I still maintain a small list of things I avoid, such as movies that show women being tortured. I do not think that my life is less rich because I do not allow myself these images, and perhaps no one should allow these into their lives.

I have almost completely overcome my claustrophobia. A little bit of discomfort is quite a victory over a full-blown panic attack and passing out!

Sometimes, I do not even have discomfort. This is a great victory for me as it was always unnerving for me to be a guest in someone's home and not want to use her small windowless powder room! And who wants to walk up eight flights of stairs when there is an elevator available!

Make some heroic choices as to how well you want to heal your triggers, but do not make unreasonable demands on yourself.

For example, if you are an incest survivor, the person who committed the trauma on you might be a relative that you cannot avoid 100 percent of the time, but you do not have to invite him/her into your home for coffee and cake and a chat.

I have pretty much gained some victory over all my triggers, except one that I choose to hold on to. Because I was abducted, control is a huge issue for me. Any amount of selfish control, even a tiny amount of someone seeking any kind of control over me might trigger a response of anger in me.

Most of the time, I can just walk away from a controlling personality with disgust. But if I feel that someone is actively trying to exert their will and agenda into my life, such as deciding for me who I am, how I feel, where I can work, where I can live, exercise my religion, spend my money, or any rule over my personal life, they are in for a fight.

People who start a conversation, looking me in the eye, with the two nasty accusing words, "You should," should be ready with a place to hide and hope I can't find them. There is a little exaggeration here, but you get the picture: I will not be controlled by anyone but God.

This is one trigger I have chosen not to get rid of, just a bit of modification sometimes if I am quite certain the other person means me no real harm. In my mind, this attitude keeps me safe from predators that want to take what is not rightfully theirs. I have learned that not all predators will physically harm you, some may emotionally do harm and I consider them a threat also.

No one has a right to take even a few minutes of my precious life that I can never get back. I am certain that most trauma survivors feel the same way.

Through time, I have learned to modify my anger at a controlling personality. I do not consider myself to "not be nice" if I do not put up with someone else's selfishness. I have erected good boundaries, which I will discuss in more detail in another chapter. Usually now, I contain my anger and process it at a later time while I politely excuse myself and think of a good exit strategy.

"Huggy" people make me nuts. If you are my immediate family or close friend, a hug is welcome. If I am not close to you, the touching makes me uncomfortable, and I have talked to many survivors who feel the same. I trust that most people reading this can identify with these feelings.

I have grieved the loss of the things I cannot get back while I was under someone else's control. I have chosen not to continue to grieve over those things anymore.

Summary of the Action Plan

Identify the losses and write them down.

1. Break down each loss into specific points.

2. Grieve each point.

3. Set a time limit on each point. (Some may take longer do what you need.)

4. Identify the triggers associated with each point, or in other words, figure out the people, places, and things that make you feel as if the experience is happening again.

5. Choose a plan of action to cope with or eliminate the triggers.

Pray and ask God to help and show you how to cope with each point effectively.

Do not take on the whole trauma at once. It would be overwhelming. Look at one offense or point one at a time and deal with it for a time and move on to the next.

God will give you the strength you need, just ask him. He will give you the answers you lack, just ask Him.

Part of being a victim is feeling powerless. By actively doing the action plan and bathing all of it in prayer, you should slowly begin to feel as if you are taking back your power. If you diligently do your action plan, you should start feeling like a survivor and not like a victim.

Built into the action plan is a way to help you rid yourself of the victim mentality that has plagued so many of us.

And then, go do something you enjoy. You will need to get your mind off this at times. Doing the grief work actually requires a balance of doing things that bring you happiness and joy. Have some fun today.

> Blessed is the man that trusteth in the Lord, and whose hope the Lord is. For he shall be as a tree planted by the waters, and that spreadeth out her roots by the river, and shall not see when the heat cometh, but her leaf shall be green; and shall not be careful in the year of drought, neither shall cease from yielding fruit. (Jeremiah 17:7–8)

1. Read Deuteronomy 34:8 to remind yourself that there is a time we should all appoint to stop grieving and move on with our lives.

2. Read Psalm 148.

3. Ask the Holy Spirit to help you identify your losses and triggers. I could give you examples, but then, I may miss an important area of your life or you may mistake one of the problems for your own. The Spirit of God is your best counselor here. Pray earnestly for the answers, and when the time is perfect, I trust that He will guide you and give you all the answers that you need, sometimes from unexpected sources.

4. This may be a time of night for you, sing in the night. Make a joyful noise unto the Lord all ye lands (Psalm 100:1).

8

Boundaries

It was a warm sunny Colorado summer day with not a cloud to be seen. The weekend was upon me, and I decided to get some things done that I had been putting off.

The day before, I had decided to do some intense cleaning, and putting on a comfortable sloppy old pink dress (very suitable for bending and moving freely) and tying my hair into a tatty old scarf, I was now ready to get dirty and work hard.

As I tackled nasty closets and dirty shelves, the nice day beckoned and I felt the urge to be outdoors. I slipped on a pair of old chore boots, because they were right next to the door, and walked out into the lovely day.

My eyes scanned our beautiful property's outdoor landscape, and then I spotted a curious sight.

Our stallion was housed in a northeast ten-acre pasture that day, and he was very agitated. More careful observation told me why he was in such a state.

There beyond his pasture was a small herd of horses. I immediately felt sorry for their owner. Here were five horses having fun on hundreds of acres of public land and they could be hurt or stolen because there were no boundaries (fences) to protect them.

Then the awful realization hit me. These were *my* horses!

In a partial panic, I ran to the tack room and grabbed the first halter and lead rope I saw. I did not need other halters and ropes for all the horses; experience taught me that I only needed to catch the lead horse. Every herd of horses has an alpha leader, and when you catch that horse, all the others will follow.

Our horses were up on the rocky mesa now and a two-wheel drive vehicle would be useless if I wanted to drive out to them, so I set out on foot with a determined stride. The herd was only about three-fourths of a mile away from the ranch, so I knew I could walk the distance.

Not to be left out, the dogs and even a few of the cats decided to follow after me.

Loose animals give their owners anxiety because of the potential harm that can come to the animal. They can be stolen, of course, but they also can be hit by a car or injured with no one to help. In our area, mountain lions are also a problem. Although a lion will seldom attack an animal the size of a full-grown horse, if the horse should become lame or hurt in some other way, he could become a target for a big cat, and we have plenty of big cats here.

I slipped the halter onto Spike, the alpha horse, and led my animals back to the safety of the ranch. I drew a big sigh of relief, knowing that soon I would have them back in proper boundaries.

I know I looked to be quite a silly sight in my unfashionable dirty clothing and big boots, leading a herd of horses followed by three dogs and some cats. Just how insane the whole picture looked was confirmed when a carload of tourists happened by, hanging out of their windows, snapping pictures of us. I wonder how many of their "silly vacation shots" made it to social network pages.

As I led my animals back onto our property, I realized that there must be a fence down somewhere for all these horses to escape so neatly. They had been housed in a pasture that is roughly forty acres. I knew that this would be too much for me to investigate right then and decided to lead them into an empty pasture and wait to get the fence repaired.

Placing the horses back into the same pasture that they had just breached was not the best solution as they would just find their way back out again. I would have to wait to get the fence repaired.

This little story may not be very interesting to most people, but it does easily illustrate one truth. The truth here is that boundaries can help keep us safe and out of bother.

Boundaries are important, and if your boundaries were traumatically breached when you were young, erecting smart boundaries may be difficult for you. Even if you have moderately healthy boundaries, a discussion on boundaries may be helpful.

When I got my horses home, I again put them in an area surrounded by fences. I did not fence my horses in because I do not wish them to have fun. I do not fence them in because I am mean and want to isolate them from all the other horses of the world.

People do not build fences because they like to. Building and maintaining fence is hard work. Maintaining fences is nobody's favorite job.

We build boundaries for our animals to live in because we care for them. Inside the fence is where we can best care for them. Outside the fences on their own are potential dangers to be reckoned with. In fact, before the house for us was started, the care and well-being of the animals was addressed first.

When I caught and recovered my horses, I did not punish them. I did not scold my horses because they pushed down the fence. I just put them into new boundaries.

I have learned to think of the Ten Commandments and other guidelines given by Christ as fences. If I stay within the fences, I have blessings. Outside the fences are dangers and consequences.

God did not set up commandments and boundaries because he is waiting for us to mess up where he punishes us. God set up boundaries to keep us safe in a world seemingly dominated by evil. Evil people can be anywhere in this world, and if you are one of their victims, this truth cannot be overstated. You already know that problems come to most all of us.

May I challenge you now to reflect on which of the commandments or boundaries were breached which caused your trauma.

It is true that killing, stealing, adultery, and lies are some examples of sin. Sin will always be wrong. If you think of the commands not to do these things as fences or boundaries set up to keep you safer, the concept of rules takes on a deeper spiritual significance.

When I think of commandments and rules as boundaries set up to keep me safe from consequences, I see a loving, caring God. God did not give commandments because he did not wish us to have fun. He set the boundaries because he knew that when we breached them, there would be natural consequences to pay (not punishment, that is another subject entirely), and he does not like to see us pay the consequences.

I recently heard a story of a young girl that had a big crush on a good-looking boy. To impress the boy and her girlfriends, she told a lot of lies. The boy found out and would not speak to her again. The girl cries and laments and hurts terribly.

The girl broke the boundaries. The word of God says that we should not bear false witness, and lies are not okay. Did God punish her? No, God did not punish her, she punished herself when she breached the boundaries, and the boundary here is not to tell lies. If she had stayed within the boundary of truth, she would not have had to experience the pain.

As a parent, I set up many rules for my children. Not once did I give them a rule because I did not wish them to have fun. I made rules to keep my kids safe.

I am not going to pretend that following all the rules ensures that we will *never* get hurt.

Coyotes breach the fences to carry off my lambs, no matter how hard I try to keep them safe. Sickness sometimes comes to my animals, the weather can be brutal, and any number of things can happen within the fence, but bad things are more likely to happen outside the fences than inside them.

It is very likely that you have had your boundaries breached like I have. We did not ask for these things and probably, most of us who have suffered severe trauma, were well within the fence when the wolf came to take us. This is when we subconsciously get confused about boundaries. Many survivors subconsciously think that they have no right to erect boundaries because of what happened to them. Sometimes we automatically just let the wolf back in because our fences were breached at such a young age, we grow up thinking we have no power to put up fences.

This is wrong thinking that needs to be changed if we are to completely heal. God sets up boundaries and we can set up boundaries too.

Unfortunately, we live in a world that (for the most part) cares little about the boundaries and rights of others, but sure makes noise and has a fit when the consequences for their actions manifest themselves. I have met way too many people who are angry about the consequences they suffer when they do wrong and accept no responsibility for their actions.

On our ranch, we call these violators, fence jumpers. When we have a cow that habitually jumps over the fences, we take her to the sale. Not only is she a danger to herself, but she is also a danger to the people in the car that might hit her. It is a risk to us, who have to get a 1,300 pound cow back in the fence!

In my life, I have made many mistakes, but at my age, I now have learned never to deliberately jump the fence. No matter how "green" the grass on the other side looks, I know that when I begin to munch on it, that it is probably a thistle.

Boundaries, or fences, whatever you call them, it is best to stay within and erect them around you too. We can erect fences for ourselves because it is good to love us!

I believe that part of the journey through the prison to the gates, includes a stop at the proclamation of boundaries.

This is also an exercise that you may want to bring your therapist into. You may be allowing people to breach your boundaries without knowing you do. Your therapist might notice things that you do not about this.

Refer back to your action plan and make a column titled "Boundaries." Under the heading of "Boundaries," begin to list all of the things that are unacceptable to you. It is not only okay to set your own boundaries; it is emotionally healthy and helps the healing process along. Your boundaries may be different or the same as mine, but all of them are important. Think of your boundaries as a fence to protect you. Draw some crude lines to represent your fence. Label each side of the fence as a place where others are not welcome.

This exercise is actually more important than you may think. It is important for all survivors of violence, incest, rape, and verbal abuse to carefully consider boundaries, especially if your trauma happened at a young age.

It is also important to consider boundaries if you were raised with few. Some well-meaning parents do not even realize that they are teaching their children to omit certain boundaries, simply because they themselves were raised without them.

For example, hatred and bigotry can be instilled in children that are living with caregivers that have no "boundaries" on their tongues.

Alcoholism, anger, and unrest can be instilled in children who have always lived in a home where the boundaries of self-control were nonexistent.

As my journey through the corridors of healing progressed, God showed me a very important truth: Forgiveness and relinquishing anger toward the perpetrators is almost impossible till boundaries for the future are set into place.

The reason that boundaries usually need to be in place before forgiveness is given is simple. Unforgiving and anger stay in place to (in our minds) keep us safe.

We think that if we never forgive, then "they" cannot do it to us again, thus making us feel safe.

Everyone who has ever been cheated on by a spouse understands this easily. The first thing the wounded spouse does is set boundaries for the future. When the wounded party is satisfied that the other fully understands and is willing to respect the boundaries, forgiveness can freely take place.

Here are my boundary lines. Inside the four-sided "fence" is *me*.

Manipulation
Lies
Envy
Underhanded criticism
Selfishness   ME
Hateful mocking
Control
Disrespect

Each part of my fence has a name of a negative behavior that I do not allow others to do to me. They cannot come into my pasture. If they try these things, I forgive them, but I do not trust them, and I make sure that my invisible fences are all in good order when they are around.

If anyone persists in offending me by continually trying to jump my fences, I keep them outside my fence (life). Yes, anyone can be redeemed, but the trust has to be earned back. I see no place in the Bible where God commands us to blindly trust someone who wants to breach our boundaries. I have read the Bible cover to cover many times and I just don't see it.

I am happy to say that most people will just respect your boundaries and have their own boundaries that are similar to yours. A few, however, will selfishly insist on jumping your fences and munching on whatever they choose. Your boundaries must hold up. It matters not, if the fence jumpers are coworkers, friends, neighbors, or even family. Fences are fences and are erected to keep you safe.

I feel the need to add here that if your fence jumper is a parent, you still have the right to keep the fence up. I know that many of you reading this may have been seriously violated by a parent, it happens.

Let's be clear here that the commandment where God tells us to honor our father and mother does not refer to abuse. God does not say that sin against you is okay because your father is the one doing it! That attitude is blasphemy against the scripture.

If these things are a problem for you, you need to discuss this with your therapist also. If the parts of your fences are the same names as mine, might I remind you that these things are sins against you. They are sins against who you are and who God wants you to be. It matters not at all if the fence jumper is a parent or even a child of yours or a spouse, sin is sin, and God loves you too much to condone sin against you. Keep your fences up. The previous example of boundary fence that I have shown may not be the same as yours. You might even have *more* fences! The point here is to love you enough to decide what is acceptable and what is not.

A boundary for you might be labeled "guilt." Perhaps you have someone in your life who knows how to "guilt" you into uncomfortable situations. You may not have to break your relationship with these people, just do not allow them to guilt you anymore. This takes skill and practice, but once you are proficient in the art of being guilt free, no one will be able to use guilt to manipulate you. Ask your therapist to help you recognize the tactics, or take a pen and begin to list the tactics of guilt on your action plan. If you recognize the tactics in advance, it will be easier for you to avoid conflict.

You may need your therapist's help to identify not only guilt, but manipulation, control, lies, and other tactics too numerous to mention here. These kinds of people are good at what they do and you need to develop skill to deal with it without getting upset and feeling guilty for not letting them do it!

Unfortunately, someone who has been traumatized, for some strange reason, can live as though this kind of treatment of them is okay. I had few boundaries for so many years, and when I first started erecting them, it felt strange. This actually is a direct result of what abuse does to a person. Undoing the attitudes and habits that break down your fences is very healing.

At first, identifying and standing up to behavior that threatened to breach my boundaries was difficult to see, but as I continued to practice it, erecting boundaries became very easy.

When I first started practicing the art of saying no to negative behavior (erecting fences), I can tell you I encountered a lot of angry opposition. If you have been allowing others to treat you so badly for so long, they get used to it and do not wish you to change into healthy behavior. They were used to the old you. They could manage the old you, and now they will have to learn to manage the healthier you!

Action Plan and Assignment

1. Draw a fence on paper and name each fence part with the negative behaviors that you will not allow into your pasture, like the previous example.

2. Read Psalm 91.

3. Continue on with the action plan of chapter 6 if you have not finished it, which is as follows:

   A. Identify loss.

   B. Break it down into specific points.

   C. Grieve each point.

    D. Set a time limit to grieve.

    E. Identify the triggers and make a plan to cope with or eliminate the triggers.

4. Remember to keep singing praises in your night: Bless the Lord oh my soul and all that is within me, bless His holy name (Psalm 103:1).

9

Fighting

When I finally decided that it was time to get serious about healing and moving on with my life, I faced many obstacles, all internal. As I read scripture, I realized that so much of the time I was just fighting for the "right" to stay damaged. I thought I had a right to anger, hostility, vengeance, and more. Yesterday was a very difficult day for us. The morning started out normal enough. Mark went out to check our cattle herd and I headed out to the vegetable garden.

I was halfway through the weeding and watering when Mark came back motioning to me in a way that I knew we had trouble.

Quickly, I gathered the two kittens that were playing in the garden and secured them in a safe place. I ran into the house and exchanged my garden clogs for sturdy shoes, grabbed my leather gloves, and joined Mark. My husband informed me that Fuzzy was in labor, having a difficult time, and needed our help. The "our help" part alarmed me. Mark has assisted a countless number of animal moms give birth without any help from me. If he needed my help now, this must be serious.

Fuzzy was born on our ranch. We bought her mom from another ranch nearby, and when the purchase was made, Fuzzy was on the way.

Our cattle herd was primarily red and black Angus, so imagine our surprise when Fuzzy was born, long-haired and fuzzy. Clearly, someone's Scotch Highland bred bull had come through a fence one day and said hello to Fuzzy's mom.

Fuzzy was the cutest calf I had ever seen, and Mark and I had always called her Fuzzy.

We drove the truck out to the field where Fuzzy was lying.

Usually, a cow in labor will lie on her side and quietly bring her own offspring into the world quickly and efficiently, but on occasion, someone will need help.

Every cattle rancher knows what to do in these situations. Usually, the cow will lie there and allow the cattleman to assist her in the birth, and every good cattleman knows just what to do to help the mom and make the birth a bit less stressful and faster. Unless the calf is breech or some other complication, a vet is not needed. The cow does most of the work, the calf emerges front feet first, and the whole process is usually done in thirty minutes or less.

This time was going to be different. As an experienced cattleman, my husband knew from the size of the emerging feet, that this calf was at least a hundred pounds. The calf was coming correctly, feet first, nose next, but it was clear that this calf would not be born without intervention from us.

A hundred-pound calf is a difficult delivery for a 1,400-pound cow, never mind a 1,000-pound Fuzzy. Experience told us that unless we helped her, mother and baby would both die. Fuzzy is generally a quiet cow with good manners and a sweet disposition. Not so this day!

Fuzzy stood up when I approached her, and the cow was clearly on the fight. She charged me and I scrambled to the relative safety of the cab of the Dodge. She charged Mark twice and even charged the truck a few times, knocking loose one of the parking lights. This was not going to be easy.

We waited for about fifteen minutes, hoping that Fuzzy would reconsider her situation and allow us to help pull the calf into the world, but she was clearly insisting on having her own way, even if it was the wrong way. As I watched this disturbing morning unfurling, I thought of how often we as humans insist on doing it our own way, even when the way we choose will prolong suffering and keep us miserable.

Despite her awkward condition, Fuzzy stayed on the fight. This was proving to be even more difficult as she stood up and made her way farther down the field toward the trees.

We had to do something different, fast! I knew that there was a good chance that we had lost the calf, but I also knew that unless it was born soon, we would lose Fuzzy too. She would die a slow and painful death, and the calf would never be born.

Our animals are all part of our family. We had to save Fuzzy whether she liked it or not. A veterinarian would not be here for hours. We didn't have hours.

In almost any situation, cattle will respect a horse. Mark quickly saddled our stallion and decided that the only way to remedy this situation was to tie Fuzzy down so she was still, and she could not throw a kick that can easily kill a human.

If we waited till she was too exhausted to fight us, the chances of losing her were great. We must do what we could. Mark got a rope on Fuzzy, and after she was secured, the calf was pulled. To our disappointment, the calf was stillborn, but with such a difficult birth, we expected as much. The calf was a hundred pounds, just as Mark predicted.

My husband loosed the tied Fuzzy, and she stood up, still on the fight, guarding over her stillborn infant.

Mark closely watched her for a while. I watched from a distance, astride our stallion (the safe place to be). We waited till we knew all was well with Fuzzy, then we left mother to say good-bye to her baby. We could collect the calf later. Today, Fuzzy is with the rest of the herd, very normal and we are relieved. It was a disappointment to lose the calf, but we are glad we still have her.

I am sure that Fuzzy has no clue that without the intervention of the experienced cattleman, she would not be joining the herd today. If only she had surrendered to us sooner, we could possibly have saved the calf, but surely, we could have saved her a lot of extra pain and grief. If she had only trusted us, she would have not been so traumatized.

As I watched Fuzzy yesterday, I thought about humankind. I thought about those of us who have endured horrible trauma. I thought about how we humans fight against God sometimes.

I thought about how many times in my life that I fought and charged and cried and fought some more, instead of just allowing the wisdom of God to reign over the situation. I chose to fight instead of choosing his wisdom.

I thought about how many times I had been "on the fight" about my circumstances, instead of just trusting my heavenly Father and allowing him to help me. I thought I had all the answers. I did not have all the answers, but I was not asking God, who did have all the answers.

I found that it is best when circumstances get tough; instead of running from the safety of God's care, it is better to be calm and allow him to take over the situation.

Praying and asking for his intervention instead of fighting on my own has proved to be much smarter. Letting his Word comfort me and asking him to bring about the much needed solution is much better.

I think that too often we are fighting God and going into battle with the devil on our own. Too often, the battle is almost lost before we do the obvious and trust God and cry to him for help.

God is there for us always. He never promised that we would not have difficulty in this life, but we can always rely on a loving, caring, gracious heavenly Father to be there for us in the good times and the bad. We need to trust Him.

Sometimes, the battle is so furious that we cannot see the hand of God in it.

There have been many times when during problems, I have been angry (on the fight) with God. These times have definitely not been the smartest times of my life.

At those times, I demanded to know why this is happening to me! Haven't I suffered enough! Remember what happened to me at five? Did I do something to deserve this trial?

I was so mad at God that I think sometimes the trial was longer simply because I did not humble myself to accept his peace and solutions. Like Fuzzy, I was fighting with the one who had the answers to shorten and remedy my situation! I have learned to trust his judgment enough to know that he had everything under control despite my uncomfortable circumstances.

With each trial I have gone through, I have been surprised again (I am a slow learner) to find that when I surrendered my will to Him, the trial was soon relieved and sometimes even gone.

It is very common for survivors to fight against God because we have been so damaged! Like Fuzzy, we are in so much pain that we are not thinking straight. We need God to help us navigate the dark corridors of tour emotions. We cannot turn away our solution. We need to trust him.

Action Plan and Assignment

1. Read Matthew 5:2–12. This will comfort you.

2. Accept the fact that God is not pleased with what happened to you but will help you navigate the corridors to the gates of emotional freedom.

3. In spite of uncomfortable circumstances, we *can* do the tasks. Read Philippians 4:13.

10

A Different Kind of Prayer

The Word of God instructs us to pray without ceasing. I think most people think that means have a daily prayer or, maybe two or three times a day, a set time to talk to God.

Have you ever sat down to pray and think, *What do I say now? I have asked for forgiveness, praised my God, said thanks...have I forgotten anything? Have I forgotten to say thank you for anything in particular? Maybe not. What about...? No, covered that subject...oh yes, Lord, please help the lady I met yesterday...what was her name? Oh well, help her anyway please. Did I remember all my family? Checklist of people...did I forget...I should write these things down!*

About this time, the mind wanders to the sports scoreboard, what color to paint the kitchen, Saturday night events, the Little League meetings, what's for dinner, the mother-in-law's demands, what kind of car to buy, and any number of insignificant things that you are no longer talking to God about. You are not praying now, you have not been praying for a while, in fact you forgot what you were even praying about in the first place. Time to go back over the mental checklist of what you are supposed to be talking to God about in the first place.

I used to struggle with this almost every day, and it left me feeling guilty and stupid. Shouldn't I be more spiritual than this? What was wrong with me? Am I like the disciples in the Garden of Gethsemane, who could not watch and pray for even one hour?

Why is prayer so difficult sometimes? Have you noticed that prayer is never difficult when you are asking God to relieve a really big problem? Our minds never seem to wander when we are begging to heal a child, pay a bill, intervene in a big problem at work, give us a job, ease our pain or any other intense trauma or hurt. The Bible tells us that Abraham walked with God. I bet he never had problems talking to God about anything. I bet his mind never wandered to the subjects of gardening or decorating when he was kneeling in prayer. I decided that Abraham must have been far more spiritual than I am. I pondered this problem for many years, feeling guilty. I wanted a better prayer life, but how do you really talk to an almighty God?

I have listened to some people say that they pray for a parking spot at the mall.

I wondered, is God really interested in parking places? Isn't He too busy running the universe and keeping the planets in line? Does he really have a special branch of angels who are in charge of parking places?

The Bible teaches us that God is all-knowing and present everywhere. Our tiny minds cannot really grasp a concept that big, but I can accept it anyway. I can talk to God about anything anytime. What a marvelous revelation! I thought, if know people who talk to him about something as trivial as a parking place, can I talk to Him about my feelings? I decided that feelings are not as trivial as parking places and thought I would give it a try.

As I pondered the thought of talking so intimately with God, I wondered why I could not talk to God in the same way I talk to my therapist. I wondered, does He really want to know about when I feel lonely, frustrated, irritated, insecure, frightened, betrayed, or any number of emotions that I never thought to talk to Him about? Were those subjects covered by a special branch of heavenly beings as well? Is God really interested in all intimate and trivial details of my life? Then I realized that feelings are not trivial. Feelings are a big deal, and as I searched the scriptures more, I knew that my Lord is interested in how I feel. I thought about the Lord's Prayer where Jesus instructed us on how to pray. I have always used that as a model. I have always thought of the Lord's Prayer as an outline to make sure I have covered all the important things I need to talk to God about. But aren't my feelings important?

My children's feelings are important to me.

Surely, my feelings are just as important to my heavenly Father. I decided that maybe I could talk to my God on a more intimate level. I just wasn't sure how to talk to God on a more intimate level. Prayer meetings in church never seemed to be so intimate. We ask for intervention, but I never remembered praying about our feelings in church. Could I have missed it? Isn't He supposed to already know how we feel? Maybe this is why we do not talk to Him about how we feel because he already knows? Do we really want to waste God's time talking about something he already knows? Then I thought, He already knows about our sick children, finances, car troubles, and unsaved family. We talk to Him about those things. Why not talk to Him about how we feel?

When I talk to my family or friends about how I feel, I feel closer to them. I have just invited them into my inner circle of emotional intimacy. Would I feel closer to my heavenly Father if I talked to Him about how I feel? Those of us with deep traumatic hurts have a portfolio of feelings that if put down on paper, may be inches thick, if not feet thick! This is why talking to a therapist helps. We can talk about all those feelings of helplessness, betrayal, fear, and pain without feeling vulnerable.

The news flash here is that we can talk to God about all those feelings also. He loves us, He will listen.

As I have stated before, talking to someone that you feel secure with, about all those negative feelings is helpful. The best listener in the universe is God! We can talk to God about all of our feelings of trauma, but He is also interested in our day to day feelings of joy, peace, irritation, and all the other emotions that humans experience. I have learned that He is really interested in these subjects and that they are in no way assigned to a "special branch."

I learned that it is okay to tell God how disappointed I feel when a so-called friend says something unkind. I learned that it is okay to tell Him how disappointed I feel when anything does not go as planned or anticipated. He is there to comfort.

Sometimes, if I disagree with my husband, I announce to Mark that I am telling God on him! Mark is so used to this, that once in a while I do not even say it, he gets real quiet then tells me that he knows I will be telling God on him for the disappointment that he just gave me. Then we both usually laugh.

When I started communicating with God on a more intimate level, I noticed little things going better in my life. Day to day occurrences seemed to be easier if I had been talking to God on this higher level.

I remember the first time, decades ago, that I told God how I felt and asked for some small object. It was a time when I was feeling vulnerable and emotionally spent. Finances were not so good at this time. Money was tight.

A week or so later, I was in the mall, shopping for the children when I spotted an interesting looking dress and, being female, decided to check it out. I loved the dress. It would look perfect on me! The fabric was yummy and the color was perfect for my complexion. The price, however, was so far out of my budget that I did not even try it on. I thought about making one like it, as I am an accomplished seamstress, but knew I could never find that fabric.

Money was so tight at that time because of illness in the family, which brings on diminished finances. In practical terms, I knew the dress would never be mine, even though I needed new clothes badly.

That evening, after I put my children to bed, I did something I had never done before. I told God in great detail how I felt. I told him how I felt about looking shabby in church. I told him how I might feel in some new clothes. I thanked him for the roof over our heads and food to eat, and with our diminished weekly salary, I felt grateful. I told Him how good I would feel in that new dress and how disappointed I was that I could not buy it. I asked him if He could save the dress for me and put it on sale at half off, then maybe I could save enough out of the household expenses to afford the dress.

Weeks passed and I forgot about the dress until I had occasion to pass the store again, and there was the dress, in my size, the only one left, and 70 percent off! I was so excited and bought my dress, knowing that my heavenly Father was listening to my feelings.

The next Sunday, I put on my new dress and could not wait to tell everyone in church about God's wonderful listening ear! I received compliments on my dress and told each lady my story. How shocked and disappointed I was to hear from all of them that I was wrong. I was told that God doesn't do that, and it was just a coincidence. I was told that He does not listen to such frivolity.

The women who did not comment just looked at me like I was nuts. I knew in my heart that they were wrong, didn't I?

I went back to praying about the basics, forgot about the dress, and about talking to God about my feelings. All those people said I was wrong, I could not possibly be the only one right, could I?

Some years went by, and money was a little tight again. I wanted a new coat. This was many years ago, when Mark was a building contractor, and before we bought the ranch.

There was a downturn in the building industry, and with that, we had many extra unexpected bills come our way. I did not really need a new coat, I just wanted one. I was feeling just a little blue and even complaining a bit.

For the first time since God gave me the dress, I remembered the details of how I acquired it. I also remembered all those ladies that told me it was a fluke and that God was not in the dress sale business.

But times were tough on many levels, not just financial, and my feelings were raw about so many things. We were not by any means poor. We lived in a beautiful five-bedroom home on almost four acres. We were not hungry by any means and, in fact, lived in a prestigious area. Finances were not really too tight, just down a bit, a building contractor never has a predictable income.

I had just passed my state real estate exam and was now licensed to sell real estate. Things were not really so bad, I just felt bad because of lots of little circumstances.

I had just finally started dealing with my childhood trauma. Before that, I would pretend it did not happen or just keep my mind busy with something else. I had been in therapy for about a year and was now dealing with some pretty nasty stuff. I was nowhere near the healthy stage, just the hurting, spill your guts, puke out the icky stuff stage. I felt bad.

I thanked Him first and then talked to God about how bad I was feeling. I told him that a new coat might make me feel better. Yes, I could go to town, pick one out, and put it on a credit card, but I did not think that was wise.

My conversation was really not so much about the coat, but was about my feelings. With all the therapy I was going through, I was having a tough time. Facing the truth is never easy when you have lied to yourself for so many years.

I told him how I would feel in a new coat. I told Him that I would talk to no one about this, just Him. I explained to Him that I would like something dressy in a lovely expensive-looking cream color. I said I would like something professional looking, so I would look the part when I started taking clients around to look at houses. I told Him that I would "feel" professional and upscale. And I would like a really warm one as winters there were damp and brutal!

Then my talk with the Lord shifted to something else. I completely forgot that I even asked for the coat. At that time, I had just been pouring out my feelings, and I am not sure that I was even that serious about the coat.

Weeks passed and I continued in therapy, dealt with flashbacks, nightmares, depression, and changed medication a few times.

Mark acquired a new contract to build a few new buildings for a client wanting commercial storage facilities erected.

I was in the kitchen preparing dinner when Mark walked in, holding up a beautiful cream color coat, draped in plastic.

I stopped what I was doing and gasped!

"Do you like it?" he asked.

I assured him that I did indeed like the coat, and he took it off the hanger so that I could try it on. The coat fit perfectly and the fabric was lovely.

"Where did you get it? I remember asking God for a coat like this a while ago. How did you know?" I asked.

"I didn't know," he replied, "the man that contracted the buildings told me to go to some of the previously built storage units and measure them, so I could get the correct measurements for the new units.

"Going into empty units without locks, I measured a few till I got to this one particular empty unit. It had no lock and was completely empty, except for this coat hanging on the far side. The guy told me that this was an unsold unit, so I assumed that no one wanted the coat, and I thought you might like it."

This happened about eighteen years ago. I still have the coat, and it is still beautiful. Every time I see it hanging in my closet, I remember my Lord who cares about my feelings.

The Word of God says that He is touched with the feelings of our infirmities. He cares for them, He feels them, and we can talk to God about them. We can tell Him about our negative feelings as well as positive joyful ones. He cares about all things, and maybe even parking places, although it is rare, maybe never, that I ask for a parking place. I simply do not have any feelings about parking places.

But every day, I have countless feelings about innumerable things, and I have learned to talk to Him about them.

A conversation with God starts out with praise, and then I might tell him that I am feeling lonely, happy, anxious, grateful, or any other number of things that I could go on for hours to talk to my heavenly Father about.

I have an hour drive to the supermarket, so most of the time I turn off the CD player because I would prefer to chat with the Lord.

If you think it would be a one-sided conversation, you would be wrong. I can hear Him talk back to me in that still, small voice, because I am listening. The Bible tells us that the Holy Spirit is our comforter, and He is speaking, if we will but listen.

After the above-mentioned incidents, I figured out that one of the reasons that God answered my prayers in such a lovely manner is because when I asked for these things, even though I was going through very difficult times, I had expressed praise and gratitude first and then presented my feelings in a respectful manner. God is not a Santa Claus; He is not obligated to give us what we want just because we demand it.

Sometimes, I pick up my Bible to read and He resumes the conversation in His Word, and then I remember that, yes, I was asking God about that recently and here is the answer or the comfort.

Sometimes, I know that he was listening because some material object I need (like the coat) or events fall into place just when I need them. I know it was my Lord because the events happened as only He could make them happen.

Sometimes, I do not get just what I asked for and am disappointed temporarily. I have learned that my heavenly Father will always find a way to let me know that he heard my feelings and understands. And always, when I do not get the specific answer that I requested, I find out later that that "thing" I wanted was not the best for me and then I am grateful that He said no.

A good father only wants the best for his children, and sometimes, the best way is not my way.

Perhaps you did not have a good father. Perhaps he was absent or abusive.

This is not the way our heavenly Father is. Our heavenly Father is the perfect father, all knowing, all loving, all caring, and always has time to listen to how we feel. We can talk to Him any time of the day or night and do not need an appointment.

I can talk to God about my feelings of people, places, budgets, vacation, clothing, books, driving routes, weather, gardening, sewing, church business friends, family, or choosing the right doctor. I can ask Him to help with all of my decisions, and when I have found that I have made a mistake, I can hear that still small voice say, "Did you ask me about it?" Then I have to admit that, I did not think to ask God for His direction in this matter.

I do not think that I have a perfect prayer life, but I am learning to "pray without ceasing" and it has helped me heal in ways that I cannot explain. I can only encourage you to do the same, and in case you missed it, yes, I did just say that prayer helps you to heal. I know this firsthand from experience.

The devil also knows that prayer will speed your healing process along and he will give you every excuse he knows to keep you from talking to God. Talking to God is a power source, and the devil does not want you to have any power, he wants to keep you miserable.

Prayer is, simply, fellowship with God.

Start your prayers with praise to God. Tell God all your feelings and ask for His advice. Thank Him for His blessings, ask for His forgiveness, then tell Him how you feel some more. Then listen for His voice. You will get better at hearing His voice as time goes on. And you will always have a better chance of hearing Him when you start your communication to Him with praise first.

When my children were small, they were much more likely to get my full and sympathetic attention if they did not start the conversation with whining and negative talk. My children always had my full attention when they started the conversation with a thank you for something and then gave me their request. Think about it for a moment, if you go to your employer with a request, is he more likely to give you his sympathetic attention if you start out with a positive word of gratitude? Would your employer immediately tune you out if you walked into his office in a huff? Would he be less likely to listen well to your request?

We have the privilege of conversing with the God of the universe.

Sometimes, we feel bad, but the Lord's Prayer given by Jesus tells us to first "hallow His name," in other words, praise Him first, then make your requests and tell Him your feelings.

When we feel bad about life, such as tough circumstances or dealing with past trauma, sometimes we do not give God the praise we should before we begin to ask for things.

I learned that the key to God's ear is first giving Him respect and praise, and when times are tough, I call it singing in the night. I have learned to sing His praise even when times are not so good, and then I have learned to tell Him exactly how I feel.

Remember Peter in prison. It was the prayers of others that sent the angel to Peter to get him out of a tough situation. Remember again that God will do for you the things you are incapable of, but all of us can pray and all of us can learn a more intimate way to communicate with our Holy God.

As you make your way to the iron gates of emotional freedom, take time at the altar of prayer.

Action Plan and Assignment

1. You should always start your prayers with praise. Read Psalm 150 to help show you how.

2. Pray and tell God how you feel about healing. Ask God for healing for you.

3. Continue on with your action plan of working through your triggers and grief and losses. Continue crossing them off your list as you move on.

4. Read James 4:3 and James 5:16.

5. Read Matthew 6:7–13.

6. Read Matthew 7:7–11.

11

You Are What You Eat

Traveling from the quagmire of trauma to the gates of healing freedom is sometimes exhausting in the extreme. As you progress through the corridors, your mind and heart require some energy.

With God, all things are possible, and if your physical health is very bad right now, God will still lead you through those corridors, but it will be easier if your physical health is good. I think we have an obligation to do what we can about our physical health too.

Remember Peter in prison: God will do what we cannot, but we are required to do what we are able.

In the past, I have done some reading on the subject of trauma and its relation to our physical health. It is my understanding that all types of trauma have the ability to affect our physical health. I am not an expert on this, but it does make sense to me.

Depression for instance (something I am very familiar with) is a whole body illness, not just sadness. Some symptoms can include chronic fatigue, insomnia, headache, digestive disorder, backaches, all over physical pain, as well as restlessness, irritability, sadness, lethargy, and a loss of interest in hobbies and pleasurable activities.

I had a wakeup call one day when I read through the list of symptoms. I did not think myself depressed because I did not feel sad. I had all the other symptoms, mainly chronic fatigue. I had an epiphany when I could see the correlation between the start of my chronic fatigue and my abduction. This, of course, prompted me to visit my doctor who confirmed the diagnosis.

Your MD should play an equally important part in your healing. Do visit your doctor with any physical problems you have, and tell your physician about your trauma.

I had other physical problems as well, and they also, could be linked back to five years old also.

I will not go into detail here about physical problems because I feel am not qualified to write about them with enough accuracy.

At five, I started feeling bad in so many ways. Fibromyalgia was a major part of my life then and was for decades after that. Chronic digestive disorders, chest pain, and other things that are not usually a problem for a child not yet six.

The doctor told my mother that these were all "growing pains." Is there really such a things a growing pains?

I am not saying that for everyone, these disorders are caused by trauma. I know that plenty of people suffer from these and more who have never experienced trauma.

We all know that stress can weaken the body in some of us, and I am one of them, and I think we all can agree that trauma is stress. My body does not stress well. I have found ways to help my system handle the stress better and alleviate some symptoms.

In 1973, I discovered some things that helped me with my symptoms and I believe made my body stronger. Today, I am even free from some things that I was diagnosed as long as I follow a few simple rules.

In April of 1973, someone introduced me to the power of natural organic foods, herbs, and supplements. This may not seem like an earth-shaking revelation to you, but trust me, in 1973, it was revolutionary. The concepts were new, and I was ridiculed in the extreme for the changes that I made in my cooking and lifestyle.

Organic food was hard to find and extremely expensive then, not as readily available as it is today. I tended my vegetable garden with new enthusiasm, knowing that the vegetables in my garden were organic and cheaper!

Through the years, as I learned more and applied more dietary principles, I saw some positive changes.

When my children were small, I was much stricter with diet than I am today, but I believe I did right. My children rarely saw a doctor or dentist and not one of the five had a single cavity until they grew up and made their own choices.

When my son was two, he was in the church nursery during service. I watched the nursery workers hand out a cookie wrapped in cellophane to each of the children. This was a very popular cookie, but John had no idea what it was. He turned it over in his chubby little hand a few times, and when he figured it was nothing to play with, he threw it down and went for the toys. The other children enjoyed their cookies.

Soda and bagged snacks were almost never in my home, and today is no exception. These things are treats, not staples.

I am an avid label reader, and even today, there are additives in certain foods that bother my system. I cannot buy these products.

Artificial sweeteners give me migraines in the extreme, so I avoid them as well as other things that I cannot pronounce. I figure that my liver and digestive system has to find a way to deal with these man-made products and that could put more stress on my body. I have had enough stress without making more for myself.

If these products are not a problem for you, then that is okay, I am just saying that I learned to pay attention to my body in relation to what I put in it. I add these statements because I truly believe that if your physical body works better, it is easier to heal emotionally. My doctor says that there is a direct mind-body connection, though I know that not all physicians agree with this. I agree with my doctor.

This chapter is in no way meant to give a full education on foods and supplements, there are whole books written on the subjects by people who know much more than I do. You may already know and practice healthy habits better than I do.

The point here is to be aware that foods and herbs can be an effective tool to help you with physical and emotional healing.

I have learned which foods not only to avoid, but which supplements to feel well and increase my energy. I take no medications now for depression and have not taken these medications for some years.

I will not go into any detail as to which supplements and herbs I take as everyone is different. What works for me may not be effective for you. What works for me may not be compatible with your medications. And please let me give a word of caution here, herbs should be considered medicines, treat them as such. The herbs I keep on hand are not meant to be taken for life.

My advice is to check out a locally owned (not a big chain, you can go to them later) health food store with a knowledgeable staff. Ask questions of the people. Do not buy herbs or supplements right away until you have done some reading and researched the products. You should find plenty of books and other information materials there as well as online.

Then before you buy, check with your doctor. If your doctor is not very knowledgeable about herbs and supplements, find one who is. When I list an herb on my medical chart, my doctor knows exactly what it is and what dose is best for me. If I am not sure, I do not start the herb or supplement till I talk to him.

When he has prescribed an herb or supplement instead of a drug, it has saved me all the potential side effects that a drug may have.

The message from me to you is simple: healthy body, better healing capacity. In my opinion, stuffing myself with chemical-laden nutritionally zero stuff and expecting me to stay healthy is the same as sitting on the busy railroad track and expecting not to get hit by the train.

I think moderation is the key here. I do love certain "not so healthy" foods, but I do not allow them to be weekly indulgences.

I save those for holidays or the movie theater, just treats, and believe me, I savor each bite!

A little self-control can go a long way. Be mindful of drug interactions with supplements and follow your doctor's instructions.

Feel as well as you can while you work out your emotional healing and get some exercise to help you work out the kinks.

Action Plan and Assignment

1. Read Genesis 1:29.
2. Keep working on the steps of your action plan.
3. Read Psalms 148.

12

You Are Fired

If you have been faithfully and diligently working on your action plan, identifying and working through your issues, reading scripture and meditating on it, I wish that I could say that you will never experience a meltdown ever again. If I promised you this, I would be lying. I stopped lying sometime in my early teens because I was so bad at it, so I may as well just tell you the truth. Perfect people and perfect lives do not exist. I am ashamed to admit it, but there are rare days when I just "lose it."

All those truths that I have previously written, I know well, but there are days (thankfully not too often) when I feel as if all the progress I have made just took a fast train elsewhere.

I do my very best to avoid all triggers, but sometimes, they are just not anything that I can control.

People and places and things change, bringing new challenges and old triggers. If I only get triggered once or twice a day, I can handle it gracefully and quite well. There are days, however, when the triggers are nonstop and multiple. Despite how much I try to look to the Lord, some days, the triggers are relentless and multiple and I am overwhelmed.

One way to deal with this is with a tool my earthy father, John, taught me. We call it, you are fired.

Some days, you just have to fire yourself so that your mind can reboot and your body can relax. The "you are fired" concept takes a little practice, but I have gotten pretty good at it.

At times, when I am overwhelmed, I tell the Lord that it is His problem, not mine, and then I go do something I enjoy. There are times, of course, that I cannot immediately go do something I enjoy. It is impossible to leave the situation if you are in traffic, in the presence of your mother-in-law, at work, or in the middle of breaking up a fight between your kids, but you can still fire yourself and tell the Lord that this is His problem and you do not care about it anymore. Tell God that He is going to have to deal with it and you do not care what the outcome may be because He is management and you are only labor.

I have always felt better when I fire myself. I know that my heavenly Father has all the tools and answers and is far better equipped to solve this problem than I am.

Now my mind can be free to think about fun things; after all, I am fired now, I can go play.

Sometimes when I fire myself, I choose a book from the shelf that I have not read yet. My whole day is occupied in the reclining chair with my book and favorite snacks. This is one of those days when healthy snacks like carrots and salad will not do. I go for the good stuff: popcorn and cherry Coke! It is a thing indeed that this only happens once or twice a year because junk food is generally not allowed, but when I am fired, I make an exception.

I don't answer the phone.

I don't answer the door.

I get in my "jammies."

I make homemade chocolate pudding.

I read more chapters.

I refuse to deal with the dishes.

I might take a nap.

I read some more.

I get to the climax of the book and refuse to put it down unless someone is bleeding or dying.

I finish the book.

I am rested and starting to get bored.

I survey the house, a bit untidy now as everyone else has to fend for themselves. But that is not my problem, I am fired today.

I take a shower, wash my hair, and give myself a manicure.

I pop in a favorite movie and watch it with some popcorn and go to bed.

The next morning, I feel well rested and have fresh new outlook on everything. I wonder why I was upset yesterday. I feel good, energized, and ready to take on the world.

If you have small babies, this type of firing is not an option, but maybe that is why God invented babysitters.

You need to come up with your own way of firing yourself. You could go golfing, give yourself a spa day, have your favorite movie marathon, ride a horse, take yourself to lunch at a really nice restaurant, play ball, play tennis, go to the gym, go to a movie, go swimming, go to the park, call friends and join whatever they are doing, go shopping (unless you have addictive spending habits). You need to come up with your best ways to fire yourself. Believe me, this is very effective. Even Jesus got away sometimes by himself. When my children were small and I felt overwhelmed, I would announce that I was fired today and then I would grab some snacks and possibly a picnic lunch, load the kids into the car, and set off for the park. We would run through the nature trails, play on the equipment, splash in the lake, and eat our snacks with lots of laughter. These actually are some of my fondest memories of my children when they were little. Imagine some of my best memories coming about because I fired myself. The housework, telephone, bills, in-laws, neighbors, and business problems would just have to go without my attention today, I was fired. I am sure you could think of many more things to do. Do not think about your problems or whatever is triggering you, think about playing, you are fired for now.

There have been times when my fired days were spent driving and wandering. If I saw a fair, flea market, or anything else that caught my attention, I would stop at those functions, just enjoying my own company. The day was all about me. Sometimes, a bicycle ride that took most of the day was just what I needed. These days, my favorite way to fire myself is to go out into my studio and sew. Whatever you choose to do, just remember that this will not work unless you have successfully fired yourself for now.

Next time life seems overwhelming and the triggers are coming nonstop, just fire yourself. I am confident that if you try it you will like it. For me, the overwhelming days do not came as often, I think mostly because I have learned to handle most things by telling God right away that this is His problem and I will just let His marvelous managerial skills take care of it. I can usually fire myself from the problem before it gets to me.

Unfortunately, there have been times through the years when the stress multiplies itself daily. There are times for all of us when a stressful situation might turn into weeks or months. We all face times when a loved one's prolonged illness, negative marriage situation, job stress, loss of a job, or any other negative things crawl into weeks, months, or sometimes years.

I have to admit that during my times of prolonged stress, I sometimes have had to go back to the doctor for medication. These stressful times for those of us who are survivors can be far worse because usually, with stress comes triggers. If you take a "step back" and lose your temper, lash out at someone, go back to therapy or your doctor, do not feel guilty.

After you calm down and analyze what caused the meltdown, ask yourself what was really going on?

What triggered you?

Who triggered you?

Tell the Lord how you felt about the situation and ask Him for forgiveness and a solution. However, if you have battled with drug addiction, medication may not be the best solution. Pray about it, and then talk to your doctor.

Some situations such as the illness of yourself, or a loved one, could require some very creative firings, if only for an hour or two. Remember to tell God how you feel about the stress Perhaps you need a change. If the job is your prolonged stress and it constantly triggers you, tell God how you feel and ask for a new job.

If your big stress is family that you have no control of, ask God to intervene in the situation. You might be able to avoid certain family members altogether. You can keep praying for them, of course, but if your stress is a family member who abused you, you do not displease God by avoiding them permanently or in part. I can forgive people without having fellowship with them. If they have not repented of their deeds, how can you have fellowship? Satan loves unrepentant family members because they can be used as triggers to keep hurting you. I know that there will be those people who say that you must stay in the situation so that you can be a witness and testimony for God. That may be, but few of us are strong enough to do that without being relentlessly triggered and in deep emotional pain. If the triggering and pain is where you are right now, your attempt to bring family members to the Lord could be futile.

If these family members trigger you so badly that you are having meltdowns more often and having your doctor strengthen your medication, my advice is to separate yourself as much as possible, at least for a time. Tell God how you feel about this, He will understand your pain.

Moving to another state is a great way to separate yourself. You can talk to them once in a while on your own terms, and have a perfect excuse to miss family functions that would keep you in extra therapy for weeks, long after the family function has passed.

Although they never asked, I feel in my heart that I have let go and forgiven my abductors, but since they never repented, I certainly would not invite them into my house for coffee, pie, and a chat. I know that there are people who could even be "friends" with a former abuser, but I know that I could not be friends with an abuser who has not repented. If you are one of those who can be friends with an unrepentant abuser and you do not get triggered, then by all means attend the functions and God bless you, my friend!

I suffered tremendously at the hand of Satan worshipers, but I think I had it easier than those of you who had a father or mother who abused you in similar ways. I think you have had a more difficult time than I did, simply because these people are your family.

I have talked to other ritual abuse survivors who have their lives threatened by family members. I have talked to people in hiding because their own mother and grandmother would literally murder them for pulling away from devil worship. To all of you in that situation, my advice is to tell God how you feel about this, stay in hiding, and pray for the salvation of your family.

By all means, do not feel guilty for taking care of yourself emotionally by avoiding certain situations.

Guilt is a very nonproductive emotion and one of the favorite tools in the devil's tool belt to make us feel miserable. Do not let him use guilt on you. God would never guilt you into a situation that is so uncomfortable and painful, if you are not ready to handle it. He loves you more than that. Yes, the Lord has promised to take care of us, but if I stand in the middle of an interstate highway and jump in front of a semi, all the while declaring that God will take care of me, there is a real good chance that I will leave the highway in a body bag. We need to use the common sense that God gave us. In conclusion, remind yourself that you are human. Do your best but do not beat yourself up when you forget the healing principles you thought you knew well. You are progressing through the prison corridors, and sometimes, you might stumble in the dark. Ask God's forgiveness, dust yourself off, fire yourself for a while if you need to, then forgive yourself, and move on.

Action Plan and Assignment

1. Continue on with your action plan.

2. Read Matthew 10:29–39.

3. Read Psalm 149 and remember to praise the God who saves you, and even if today feels like the blackest night, sing in the night by praising God and you will feel better.

13

I Am Afraid

While going through the corridors and looking for the gates of healing, sometimes I have been afraid.

Fear is something that plagues a survivor's life, but with practice in trusting God, we can gain victory over the crippling effects of fear.

One minute, I felt safe and innocent, the next minute, I was in terror. I never really experienced fear before my abduction, but after, fear was a daily part of my life. The lovely lie that says it cannot happen to me did no longer apply to my life. I then knew that bad things could happen to me. This intense fear was part of my daily thoughts until I learned to deal with it.

Trauma survivors are usually battling fear, especially if they are PTSD. Fear in the form of flashbacks and nightmares are common, but the hourly wariness of what could happen is even more damaging than flashbacks and nightmares. It is something that a survivor of intense trauma might deal with every day.

Fear was hurting my life even more than the initial trauma because, in a way, I was r-experiencing the abduction all over again. My whole life revolved around the happening when I was five years old and manifested itself in looking over my shoulder, being wary and suspicious, and expecting the worst to pop out and grab me at any minute.

New people, new buildings, new experiences, new anything, was great anxiety for me. Everything I did, saw, touched, and tasted had the potential to cripple me for the day, week, month, or year. I think I hid this pretty well from most people, but I know that the effects of being afraid of everyone and everything were not good. This was especially difficult before I sought therapy because I had no one to bounce my fears off of. I just kept all these fears buried as far as I could and put on a face to the world that I was fine and I was not in fear, even when I was terrified. In therapy, I learned that this was pretty normal for someone who has experienced such abuse, but the knowledge that this was normal did not help me to be fearless. Therapists helped me to learn tools to deal with specific situations, but I still never felt free.

Again, I found the answers in the Word of God.

God is speaking when He says:

> I, even I, am He that comforteth you: who art thou that thou shouldest be afraid of a man that shall die, and of the son of a man which shall be made as grass; and forgettest the Lord thy maker that that hath stretch forth the heavens and laid the foundations of the earth, and feared continually every day because of the fury of the oppressor, as if he were ready to destroy? and where is the fury of the oppressor? (Isaiah 51:12–13)

For weeks and months after I discovered these passages, I read them every day. I knew that I had not previously been taking comfort from the Lord like I could have been, so my fear had been rampant. Memorizing and believing the words of the Lord was the action I needed to eradicate my chronic fear. Adding a "fear" column to my action plan was a start.

Beside each identified fear, I listed possible ways to deal with each fear. I put down beside some of them, certain scripture verses that I had come across in my daily devotional that gave me comfort.

This proactive behavior helped quite a lot, but I received real victory and comfort when I learned to make these verses of scripture part of myself. As I read and reread the passages, I absorbed their truth and they became part of who I am. Reciting certain positive things about myself helped in the process of making the truth of scripture part of who I am. My plan looked something like what follows.

Action
Positive Affirmation Plan

I am not fearful anymore. I trust in God and the Lord Jesus Christ to help me be safe. I choose to believe God and the scriptures. I choose not to allow others to cause me anxiety when none really exists. I choose a positive, proactive approach to solving my fears with affirmative talk and thinking. I do not let the devil make me cower with fear.

I know that God is with me, I am fearless, strong, and protected.

I still practice all of the physical common-sense things, for safety's sake, such as locking doors, scanning parking lots, and paying attention to my surroundings, but I am not internally crippled with anxiety and fear.

It comes down to a simplistic attitude of choice. I can choose to be fearful or I can choose to trust God. Fear does not have to be an automatic response that I have no control over. I need to practice an attitude of fearlessness, and it gets easier with time. The most difficult part of practicing fearlessness is when the fear comes on by a genuine trigger!

Now here I am talking about those nasty stubborn triggers again. I find it necessary to continue to talk about triggers because triggers are emotional responses that we do not think about first, they just attack us, like a mountain lion jumping out of a tree. We do not see it coming because we do not expect it, and the response is involuntary.

Trigger fears can be a real problem.

When I am triggered and fearful, I first think about what I am going through and identify what really triggered me. Was it a person, phrase of speech, place, picture, or anything that might place me back into the past? When the trigger is identified, I give myself some positive, affirmative self-talk about the problem.

The most effective way to do this is to remind myself that this is a trigger and not what is really happening. I am only being reminded of my past, I am not there still. This shift back to reality usually deactivates the trigger.

When going through the corridors of healing, the fear station can be a place where people get stuck for a long time if they let it.

If you think that you cannot move on from your fears, then you will not. God will give you the courage to move on from fear, but you must accept the courage. If you think you can't stop being fearful, you are choosing not to accept God's provision of courage and peace.

I learned that fear is really a choice, not something that I need live with because I can't control it. I can control it, and I do not have to live with it. I can move on. I am not completely fearless. I still get triggered sometimes, and I am a very careful person. The healing lesson here is that fear is no longer a part on my daily life that rules every decision, thought, and attitude. I no longer have that hourly wariness of what bad thing is going to happen. I am wary at times (if circumstances look strange), but I am free from the bondage of fear. I am no longer constantly jumpy.

Before, I was just fearful of everything without any reasonable explanation as to why. Now, if I fear, it is a choice brought about by nasty circumstances. For example, when I was taking a walk around a reservoir, just there for the exercise, with no fear, I became fearful when I saw two men break into and go through my car. I then became nervous and thought what to do to keep myself safe.

The story is true, and happily, the men did not find me, but the point here is that my anxiety and fear was valid, brought about by circumstance.

An example of an invalid involuntary fear would be, if no one was going through my car, but I was gripped in intense fear expecting someone to be.

Thus saith thy Lord the Lord, and the God that pleadeth
the cause of his people, behold I have taken out of thine
hand the cup of trembling, even the dregs of the cup of my
fury; thou shalt no more drink it again: But I will out it
into the hand of him that afflict thee. (Isaiah 51:22)

In your action plan and assignment, you will find an assignment
to read Psalm 37. Psalm 37 is one of my favorite Bible passages
because it has always offered me so much comfort, understanding,
and freedom from fear. Do read and meditate on Psalm 37 today
and every day.

I think sometimes people do not heed good words of advice
because they seem too simple. We sometimes think that simple
solutions have to be too good to be true! It is a simple solution
to read much of the comfort scriptures, but it really does work. I
found that reading aloud the verses does me most good, maybe it
is because I concentrate on them more, I don't know, I just know
it works. The Word of God is powerful and will always give you
what you need, that is why He gave it to us!

Psalm 91 is another passage that you should commit to
memory. Read all of Psalm 91 to get the most benefit, but I will
focus here on verses 14 and 15.

Because he hath set his love upon me, therefore will I
deliver him: I will set him on high, because he hath known
my name. He shall call upon me and I will answer him: I
will be with him in trouble. I will deliver him and honor
him. (Psalm 91:14–15)

These verses give me great comfort, but to activate them and
make them real in my life, I need to believe and trust God and
His word.

I think it is good to note here that in verses 14 and 15 that
God is speaking to us! He is telling us in the beginning of verse
14 that the prerequisite to getting the protection of God is just to
love Him. He says, "Because he hath set his love upon me."

So we know that the first way to activate the protection plan is to determine to love Him.

After we love him, he tells us that He will deliver us and set us on high, just because we know His name!

When I really let this truth be part of my soul, the whole thing seemed to be too wonderful for words. He will deliver me just because I love Him! That is all I have to do? How easy is that! My Lord is not asking anything difficult of me, He is just saying that in return for my love for Him, He will be my champion!

Just in case I forget, God elaborates on this in verse 15. He tells me that when I call Him, He will answer! He says He will be with me in trouble.

Notice here that God does not promise that I will not have trouble, what He says is that when trouble comes, He will be with me and deliver me, and He will even honor me! All I have to do is love Him, and I can do that. If fear is a problem for you, you can include things you are afraid of in your action plan. As you think of tools and things helpful to overcome the particular fears, write the above verses next to each solution. The verses of scripture are the power behind the solution. Or put another way, the verses of scripture are the ways to activate your solutions. The Word of God is very powerful. I learned not to just know about the Word, but to use it and activate it. If you still have a daily fight with fear on your hands, my prescription is this: read Psalm 91 and Psalm 18 in the morning and before you go to bed at night. I have found that a focus on the Lord before you go to sleep is the best defense against nightmares, night panics, and flashbacks.

Some fears will go away with the above prescribed suggestions, but there are those out there who may not even recognize that they have certain fears or triggers. The reason that some people may not recognize their triggers and fears is because they have used drugs, alcohol, eating disorders, gambling, shopping, or other addictions to mask their fears and triggers.

It is vitally important to identify fears and triggers if we want to completely heal, and in many cases, the addiction might be a direct response to a particular fear or trigger. Too often, we as humans will go straight to the addiction so that we do not have to feel the effects of the fear or the trigger.

Getting to the bottom of our hidden fears and triggers can be the magic pill that ends some addictions. Learning what triggers our addictions can be hard work, and sometimes, it is a marvelous epiphany that may end the cycle. Everyone is different, but it is important to look carefully at whatever addiction we have, including the addictions of perfection and anger, and learn what triggers them.

Action Plan and Assignment

1. List your fears on your action plan and get creative with ways to eliminate the fear. If you need help with this, bring your action plan to your next therapy session. List the appropriate scriptures next to you fears when you find a verse that fits.

2. Until you find verses that fit your particular fears, use Psalms 91 and 18. Read these Psalms twice a day.

3. Read Isaiah 51 verses 12 through 22.

4. Read Luke 12:4–7.

5. Say some positive words of affirmation for yourself (positive affirmation plan).

6. Choose to be fearless in your heart. Read 1 John 4:18.

7. Read Psalm 37.

8. On a separate sheet of paper, divide the paper into two columns. In the first column, list your addictions. Right next to your addictions, in the second column, identify the things in your triggers and fears that usually result in your addictive behavior.

14

Surrender and Grateful

The only way to eradicate a negative is to kill it with a positive! Severe trauma can lead to so many negative emotions, decisions, and consequences. If you have just started analyzing this, no doubt you are beginning to unravel and identify negative things in your life that have a direct correlation with your traumatic experience. You are possibly beginning to see certain negative aspects of your personality and life choices that can be traced back to your trauma. When one first realizes these things, they can be a trauma in themselves! What do you do about it? How do you change it? How do you stop the negative behavior and learn something new? When you begin to really see the far reaching effect of the pain you endured, you may be tempted to think it is worse than you thought! Now what do you do?

How do you begin to unravel such a mess? How do you modify your thinking and behavior now?

If you are reading this directly after your trauma has occurred, you will be blessed to know that the previous statements probably will not apply to you. The problem I was addressing is the negative personality and decision making that happens when the trauma has not been properly dealt with and ignored for years, which is when most of us finally decide to address the truth of our trauma.

We think we will just go on with life and leave it far behind, never to think about it again. Some people may be able to do that without it affecting the rest of their lives, but I think that some of us cannot achieve that goal without some thought. Let me say this, if your trauma is quite recent, do not be fooled into thinking that what has just happened to you cannot negatively affect your personality or your thinking. If you deal with it now, instead of later, you are in a position to keep the negative aspects at bay. If you put off doing your action assignments and spiritually growing in the knowledge of Jesus, you may possibly have some difficulty later with so many issues. Issues of fear, trust, and self-esteem are a few that come to my mind, so may I encourage you, not to put off having a closer walk with Jesus, using the scriptures in this book and applying the principles I have included.

If you have been putting off dealing with the truth of what your past experiences have done to your "here and now" for years, it is *never* too late to start.

The solution to this dilemma is actually quite simple, but again, it requires a conscious willingness to change the script and get through to the gates. This really is just a check station in the corridor that is a normal process. This is another aspect of your healing that will be more easily worked out with pen, paper, and your action plan.

The list of possibilities of negative actions and thought processes resulting from trauma are as follows: (I am sure you will not have *all* of them, so do not get discouraged) depression, anger, control issues, inability to connect with others, numerous phobias, hatred of the opposite sex, shopaholic, drug abuse, poor self-esteem, gossip, obsessive-compulsive disorder, shoplifter, eating disorders, violent tendencies, suicidal, perfectionist, overachiever, overreaction to small events (these are probably triggers),self-destructive behavior—example, repeatedly getting into an abusive relationship

The list actually goes on, but these examples and more are all manageable as long as they are identified. You might need a therapist's help on this, to identify all of your problem areas, I certainly did. Sometimes, these things are so ingrained in us, that we think of them as normal and healthy. I needed someone outside of my everyday life to help me identify all of my unhealthy thoughts and behaviors. It is almost impossible to change a destructive behavior if you do not recognize it as destructive and not normal.

As you compose your list, remember that this is part of your action plan and you will break it down, bit by bit, it is more manageable this way. Also, as you compose your list, remember that other's lists are just as long or even longer, you are not alone.

Now comes the hard part. The difficult part of doing the exercise is going down your list and surrendering each negative problem to the Lord. It is my experience that negatives do not go away just because we want them to. Each negative aspect of your life needs to be looked at, analyzed, and surrendered to God. This could take some time, depending on how hard you are willing to work at it. I wanted all the "nastiness" to go away so I worked very hard at it, even when it seemed painful. Just keep at it and march right down your list, it will give you a sense of accomplishment.

When you are successful at getting rid of something negative, it appears to me as if it creates some kind of vacuum. The emptiness is like a wide open invitation for more negative junk to come into your life and set up housekeeping. An example here would be of the person who quits smoking but increases eating. He may not smoke anymore, but is now eighty pounds overweight!

Negatives must constantly be replaced with something positive or the effort could be in vain. Many negatives, such as pornography and other addictions, might be simply replaced with Bible reading.

Coming up with so many positive solutions could seem impossible until you learn that there is one positive that fits all, and that is gratitude.

If you choose to argue with this wisdom and decide that you have nothing to be grateful for, you will stop your healing and get stuck at some part of the corridor till you decide to learn gratitude.

I had a difficult time with this because I was too focused on the unfair happenings in my life. It took more time to get through the corridors because I just did not want to let go. I chose for too long to decide that I could not be grateful because I had suffered too much. I learned that this was a trick of the devil to keep me from the gates of freedom. I decided to move on and learn gratitude.

I know that most of us choose not to be grateful because we feel we are owed something. We feel entitled. It seems to me that we are raising our children with that sense of entitlement.

The predominant thinking is why be grateful for food, clothing, car, home, clean running water, electricity, job, family, education, health, friends, freedom, and numerous other things? Aren't we entitled to these things?

I wonder if most people think they will be grateful when all those things are bigger and better. How big is big enough? After all, why be grateful for a Ford when what you really want is a BMW? We might think, we have worked so hard for the Ford, we earned it. Why be grateful? Now, if we won the lottery, then we would be grateful!

All of these things are owed to us, right? Wrong! None of these things are owed to us. A loving God provides so much for us that we never think to thank Him for and then we wonder why we cannot get victory over the negative effects of the trauma we have suffered.

If we are in a constant state of focus on the junk, we will never be grateful for the beauty. Gratefulness is where the blessings are, and too many of us miss the blessings because we are so involved in the past.

For way too many years, I felt that entitlement nonsense. God taught me gratitude in some very unusual but effective ways.

I had always wanted a full-time country life. I had wanted to be a farmer's wife since I was four years old. Mark and I love working on the land and everything that it represents. When we decided to sell out and go for our dream, a horrible fact slapped us in the face.

The fact is this: because there is such a large percentage of blessed people in the USA, buying up land for housing developments, second houses, and recreational ambitions, the price of farm and ranch land is unbelievable. It is not uncommon to have to spend a few million dollars for a ranch if you wanted to make a modest living off it. That is the investment needed. From that multi-million dollar investment, you just might make $50,000 per year, in a good year that is.

I could talk much more on this, but you get the picture. Unless you have relatives that pass their farm or ranch onto you, it is extremely difficult to make a living. We do not have any relatives like that so we started from scratch.

Both of us are optimists and hardworking, so we devised plans to make it work.

We knew that to make it all work, we would have to do all the work ourselves. We bought bare ground and proceeded to dig a well, build a fence, put up outbuildings, a solar electric system, and build a house. All of these tasks could not be done in a year, it took years. It took time, much more time than we had planned, but we were willing to pay the price.

It took four years, yes, I said years, to get the indoor plumbing installed! Now I always enjoyed primitive camping. We would trailer a few horses, go camping, and ride for hours, so I thought "camping" for a while would be good. It was not good. By the time the plumbing was finally installed, I was really sick of primitive accommodations. Now I do not like camping anymore.

Because we built this ranch piece by piece, I really learned to be grateful.

Things I used to take for granted and feel I was entitled to now became great blessings and reasons to thank God.

There is rarely a time when I get into the shower that I do not sincerely thank God for the indoor plumbing.

If this sounds silly to you, I challenge you to carry water for a few days. I guarantee that expressing gratitude for these things will come much easier! Expressing gratitude to the Lord for these and many other things we take for granted will be a real part of your life. It is my personal opinion that if everyone in the world practiced gratitude, there would be no more wars.

If we are grateful for what we have, then we do not covet what our neighbor has, and that in itself eliminates a lot of grief.

We were so busy chucking money into our ranch that many purchases were put on the back burner. A new car was not on the list. When we bought our ground, we owned a car that I had bought brand-new and now was paid for. Year after year, we drove this car because the money was needed somewhere else on the place. I watched the odometer go up and up, 100,000, then 150,000, and it kept climbing. A new car was not affordable because there was always a vet bill, more fences, another bred cow, and don't forget the plumbing!

Every time I got into my car, I earnestly thanked the Lord that my car was still running. Year after year went by and the odometer continued to climb. When the odometer reached the 250,000 mile mark, I figured that the engine might give up the ghost anytime, so I continued, every single time I drove the car, to sing and talk to the Lord of my gratitude.

When the car odometer said 357,000 miles, we were able to buy a new car. We sold the old car for $500 a few years ago and the new owner is still driving it! It is my personal belief that the car's stamina is directly related to all the grateful prayers I gave to God.

I now think that if I am not grateful for the blessings I have now, why would God give me more?

I know that the power of God inhabits the praise and gratitude we give Him. The first five books of the Bible are full of stories of people complaining. We can read them now and be critical of those people. We are so sure that if we had seen God part the Red Sea, that we would never be ungrateful and complaining ever again. But would we? It is easy to judge others for their shortcomings, but I think we need to judge ourselves on this matter. No, we did not see God part the Red Sea, but look around at the multitude of blessings we enjoy and never think to marvel at and thank Him for.

As I have read these five books of scripture, I realized that I am entitled nothing and neither is anyone else. I feel ashamed of the things I have taken for granted and not recognized as God's great blessings. If I have the ability to praise Jesus, this is already a great blessing. I choose to be grateful, gratitude is a choice. When I started to consciously practice gratitude and became more proficient in it, I noticed that the negative consequences of my abduction were not as bad, and some did not even exist at all anymore. A positive attitude kills a negative one every time, and there is no attitude more positive than a grateful one!

Yes, what I suffered was awful, but if I keep all the negatives that came with it on instant replay, I feel bad. I learned to turn off the instant replay by saying words of gratitude to the Lord. I did not always feel grateful, I just said the words, the feelings came anyway.

My Grandpa Rollie always used to say, "I complained about not having shoes, till I saw a man with no feet." I wish I had paid more attention every time he said that, I may have learned faster and been saved from a lot of grief.

For the past few years, I have been reading about a crisis with honeybees. It seems that they are mysteriously dying all over the world. Sometimes, whole hives are dead with no explanation.

Scientists are working on this problem, but as of this writing, I have not heard of a solution. It is not as if a bee can tell you he has a bellyache or any other symptoms, it is a difficult problem.

If all the bees go, it will mean devastation to the world food sources. Bees pollinate the blossoms that make fruit, berries, and vegetables. We would still have corn because corn is pollinated by the wind, but I think that corn could never taste like a strawberry pie.

The bees are still with us, and we all should be grateful for the bees and grateful for the food that they help to provide.

There are so many things in nature that God has provided that most of us never give a second thought to, but even if a few of these plants, animals, insects, and reptiles were gone, it may have a catastrophic effect on our lives.

When I started really being grateful for all the things I took for granted, my spirits lifted, my days were brighter, and the trip through the corridors was much easier. Practicing gratitude gave me the best look at the gates of freedom yet. I think too often we treat God as if he is a Santa Claus. We think we are so good, so we give Him a nice long list of the things we want, and most of the time, do not think to say thank you. Have you ever heard a parent instructing their child to say thank you to Santa for the gifts he brought them the previous year?

The fact that there really is no Santa is not the point, the point is that I think humanity often treats God as if he is a fictitious character, only there to grant their undeserved wishes.

I think that gratitude is more difficult for survivors because we have such epic battles with depression and anger. Anger and depression are normal responses to horrific events, but continual lifetime anger and depression leads to more misery.

Like the man I described in the beginning of this book. Not a happy prospect for those of us who have already suffered so much. You may still be dealing with anger and depression but gratitude can take a real bite out of these problems. It was in the midst of one of my bouts of anger and depression that I decided to try something new. I decided to say some words of gratitude. To say this was difficult is a bold understatement at best, as I didn't feel like being grateful.

Getting off the merry-go-round of despair, self-pity, and anger is so difficult when you see that the trauma you endured has affected more than just you. It was difficult to be the best mom for my children because my mind was so busy just trying to emotionally survive. I see vast areas of time lost with my precious children because of my own internal struggles not to go insane. Those are times I can never get back. In all areas of my life, I see large blocks of time that can never be mine again. Emotionally, I was checked out of my own life because facing the abuse was too horrible.

When I would again realize my internal struggle, I would battle with more depression and anger. I felt it was not fair, and it wasn't fair, but it was fact. I had short spurts of being grateful throughout my life, like the car incident I just related, but never had gratefulness been my main attitude for the week or even day.

It was time to try something new. It was time to make gratitude the attitude of my entire year and life. Gratitude was a choice. I did not start my "new experience" with the best of attitudes. I did not "feel" grateful. I did not feel happy. In fact, I was really angry and irritated. I did not begin to practice daily gratitude because I felt sunny and warm and grateful and life was great. On all accounts, nothing felt that way. I began to practice gratitude because it pleases Jesus and glorifies God.

As the days and weeks went by, I would express gratitude for all the things that I used to take for granted and used to think were insignificant.

I learned to be grateful that I could see. I learned to be grateful that I was not hungry. I began to be grateful that both my parents were still here to enjoy. Enjoy. What a wonderful word. I began to focus on really living in the moment and really enjoying every detail.

I started practicing how to clear my mind of past junk and focus on the beauty that the here and now give me. Little things and big things are all blessings from God. They all should be equally appreciated.

> Be careful for nothing; but in everything by prayer and supplication with thanksgiving let your requests be made known unto God. (Philippians 4:6)

Jesus showed us a simple way to show gratitude that I am afraid has gone out of fashion today. Jesus set the example when he would thank God before he ate. I think it is an example we all should follow. Our grandparents did, but today, thanking God for the food that we think we are entitled to is just not as popular as it was in grandparent's day.

I know that many people still say grace before a meal, but I wonder how many really think about what they are saying. Are they just words to recite out of some sense of duty, or is there a grateful heart behind the words? The difference is intention. If the words are truly backed up by a grateful heart, then I am sure that even a repetitious prayer is heard and loved by God.

If Jesus himself would thank God before a meal, it might be a good place to start for anyone who has not been practicing gratitude. A simple act of being grateful for food could turn into many other acts of gratitude.

It is my opinion that if more husbands and wives showed gratitude to their spouse, there would be considerable less divorce. We end relationships because we feel unappreciated, maybe God would be closer to us if we would give more appreciation! Everyone needs to feel as if the effort they make is noted and appreciated and God is no exception.

If you read the Bible cover to cover, you will find plenty of examples of God being pleased with people expressing thanks. I think we all should start by every day thanking God for the gift of Jesus who has made the way for us to attain heaven instead of eternal punishment.

Again, I will say that I think too many of us think of God in the same way we think of Santa Claus. Give me, give me, but very few words of appreciation. What I find truly remarkable is the fact that a simple act of gratitude to our Creator really benefits us! It seems like the more I thank Him, the more He gives me! When we express gratitude when we feel bad, we are truly singing in the night.

The scriptures extolling us to praise and thank God are so numerous. The Psalms are a good place to start to learn how to practice praise and gratitude. King David of the Old Testament wrote many of these while he was in the midst of his most challenging times. During those challenging times, his answer was to express gratitude.

Walking through the dark prison corridors and looking for the gates of freedom is indeed a challenging time of life.

It is my assumption that when Peter was walking through, following the angel, that he may have silently expressed a bit of gratitude that he was getting out. I know that I would have, and I bet you would have too.

It seems prudent that we can at least thank God for giving us some answers and wisdom on how to heal from our trauma. It is my personal prayer that God will help me have a full and joyful heart of gratitude!

Gratitude makes healing quicker and easier and also makes every aspect of your life easier.

Gratitude is that tiny drop of oil that makes the gears run smoothly.

Gratitude is that tiny bit of honey in your tea.

God wants us to be grateful to Him, but that little bit of gratitude makes our own life so much sweeter.

Gratitude helps me forget about trauma and troubles for a while and rejoice in life.

When an attitude of entitlement has been engraved on our DNA, it takes a lot of effort to develop a heart of gratitude. We need a heart of gratitude to grow and heal. We need to really enjoy all of the things provided by God that we take for granted.

Choosing to obey God by being grateful is one of the wisest decisions that anyone can make. Think of it as another one of your "get out of jail free" cards that you will carry with you to the iron gates. Do not linger at the station of gratitude, choose to practice it and then move on.

Action Plan and Assignment

1. Read Luke 17:11–18. This is about lepers who are healed by Jesus but not all give thanks. Note the reaction of our Lord Jesus Christ.

2. Read Matthew 12:43 Think about replacing a negative with a positive.

3. Read Psalm 150.

4. On your action plan, make a list of all the things you have to be grateful for.

5. Every day, write down five things and thank the Lord for them, list different things every day.

6. Accept the fact that gratitude is one of the choices you make that will speed your healing.

7. Think about the fact that the power of God inhabits the praise and thanks that we give Him.

8. Make a list of the negative habits and attitudes you are embracing in your life and think of which ones might me a direct response to your trauma (think alcohol, eating disorders, poor self-esteem, etc.) then, next to them in another column, write out how you can replace them with positive attitudes of gratitude.

Examples:

- Bible reading and thanking Him for His Word instead of the second piece of cake

- Praising and thanking God instead of gossiping

- Praising God and thanking Him for your best physical features and spiritual gifts instead of running yourself down with poor self-esteem

Think of many more creative ways you can use praise to create a positive in your life where a negative once existed.

Thought: If you want to see the real power of God, praise Him, and if your circumstances are difficult and dark (like the night), you will be singing in the night.

15

Rotten Apples

One rotten apple spoils the whole barrel. You do not hear this said much anymore, so I guess I am showing my age. It is a statement that I have found to be true in most cases. I am an avid gardener so this old-fashioned concept of a rotten apple spoiling the rest is practical to me.

A lot of summer produce can keep from fall till the following spring in a root cellar. In the fall, I carefully harvest my produce and arrange it in the root cellar as thoughtfully as I can, so that I can still enjoy it in the spring.

It has always been an irritation to me that only one bad vegetable or fruit can mold and spoil a whole container of good produce. Why is it that if only one bad apple can make the whole bushel of fruit spoil, that one good apple put into a bushel of bad ones can't make all of them into good fruit? Yes, I am aware of the science behind it, but that doesn't make me like to accept it!

Oftentimes, in the winter, I can be found in the root cellar, seriously engaged in a search and destroy mission, picking out disgusting bits of fruit and vegetables, so the "one" does not make the whole container spoil.

Sometimes, it is only one negative experience that can mess up a person's whole life. Some people wish that there was only one negative experience instead of a whole bushel full of abuse and pain.

Think of your trauma as that rotten apple because the concept is similar. That negative experience can ruin your whole life if you allow it to.

I told you that healing can be real work, and by now, you probably have figured out that it is also a series of choices. I am ashamed to say that the subject I am talking about now was real work for me.

The rotten apples of my previous experiences were contaminating and ruining my whole life. I had to put forth a herculean effort to apply gratitude to my everyday life. I know that I talked about gratitude in the previous chapter, but the practice of gratitude is so very vital to emotional healing that I feel the need to discuss it further.

Why is it that I can pick through a whole bushel of lovely sweet apples and the one that holds my focus is the nasty hairy squishy one at the bottom? Why am I not counting the good ones, marveling at their lovely color and shape, thinking of how good they will taste? Why am I feeling all the negative emotions of repulsion and disgust at the one, when I have dozens of nice apples?

As humans, we tend to gravitate toward the negative instead of running to the positive. If you do not believe that, then think about how much good news you hear on the nightly news. The majority of the reporting is violence and sad stories. I think that anyone that makes the statement saying, "Man is basically good," has not been paying attention. In the first place, if man was basically good, Christ would not have had to die for our sins.

I am I think a typical mother. My children were very normal. I had to teach them good behavior. Bad behavior came naturally. I had to teach them Godly habits. Nobody taught them negative habits, they figured those out all by themselves. As parents, we do not teach our children to lie, cheat, or steal. Negative behavior comes as easily as breathing and we must teach them to love God, honor their elders, respect others, give willingly, and countless other acts of righteous living. If mankind was basically good, these concepts would not have to be taught, and discipline would never be needed.

Raising kids is work, real work. If I had been sufficiently warned of how difficult it is to mold little children into good human beings, I may not have had any. I must say that all of my hard work, sleepless nights, prayers, and tears have yielded much fruit, as all of my children have become productive, beautiful people who love the Lord, and I am so proud of them, but it was real work raising them. For me, learning and practicing gratitude has been more difficult than raising my children, and as I look around at the world I live in, it does not appear that gratitude comes easy to most people. However, hard work always yields rewards and the reward of learning to look around and practice gratitude in all things can be a healed and healthy life.

You still will need to formulate and do your action plan, but remember Peter in prison, God will do what you cannot, and you must do what you can. Gratitude is a choice and we all can be grateful for something. If you are reading this, be grateful for your eyes; if someone is reading it to you, be grateful for your friend.

Unfortunately, it takes real discipline of the mind to stop focusing on the squishy rotten apples of our lives.

The conscious and subconscious rotten apples of our past cause negative thinking and bad decisions that affect the here and now. Those traumatic events that we endured play themselves over and over and manifest themselves in bad decisions, messed-up relationships, addictions, and nightmares. In other words, we might not be consciously thinking about the trauma, but the trauma acts itself out anyways unless we acknowledge that the trauma (rotten apple) may be affecting the decisions and thoughts we are thinking now.

Being thankful helps to get rid of some of the negative junk because we have switched our focus. We still have to identify the way that the trauma has affected our present-day lives, but having gratitude makes the process less painful. I will say again that tough childhoods and traumatic events can reappear in the form of addictions, relationships, and anything that can sabotage our happiness.

I now know that my abduction, torture, and rape that happened when I was five loused up my self-esteem, which attracted me to a man (first marriage) who treated me the way I already felt about myself. I hated me and so did he. Through my younger life, I can see that I have repeatedly been attracted to people who affirmed how I felt about me. Healthy relationships were uncomfortable for me, and even now, they still can be, unless I stop and analyze the situation. I remind myself that I am a good person and I deserve to have others respect me as I do them. I recognize the rotten apples before I bite into them, then I think of things I am grateful for. This simple exercise of analyzing the situation and picking out the rotten apples has been a very effective exercise for me.

Okay, so now that you understand it, how do you stop the negative subconscious thinking and move on to healthy mind-sets?

The first thing you need to do is identify all of you unhealthy mind-sets and actions. This may be simple, or it may be difficult. Some unhealthy mind-sets may have been part of your life for so many decades that you think of them as truth instead of a problem. You may need to change your truth.

This is something that I highly recommend you seek out a professional for. If you are already identifying these things, you may not need any other help. This is an area that I stopped seeing my counselor and switched to a psychologist. I am not saying that a psychologist would be more helpful to you, and I am not saying to seek other help if your current therapist is working well for you and you are making progress. I am saying that *if* your current therapist is not good at helping you pick out the rotten apples, find someone who is. It is not a matter of the former counselor being unqualified, it is a matter of you finding the right fit to help you along your way. Some therapists are really good at this, and some are stronger in other areas. I am just saying, do the best for you. This is your life, pray for God to send you the right person if your current counselor does not help you to toss out rotten apples.

If your current counselor tells you that you do not need to pick rotten apples, just do lots of affirmative self-talk, do not listen. Affirmative self-talk is very good, but remember, nice apples do not make rotten ones good. Get rid of the rotten apples.

This part of your journey through the corridors may be very difficult. You need to find the most skilled person you can. Your current therapist might be very strong in other areas and extremely helpful to other areas of healing. It is perfectly okay to see both if they are both helpful. For example, it might be helpful for you to see the therapist that helps you pick rotten apples, and at the same time be in a support group or counsel with your pastor. Use all the tools you can find to heal, but do not let anyone tell you that you do not have to figure out how that negative past has affected your present day because it probably has. This part of your healing can be so intensely painful on so many levels, but you need to do it so that the bad decisions you made that were based in your past, do not repeat themselves. An example would be of the woman that goes from one abusive relationship to another. Unless we recognize where we hurt, we sometimes keep repeating it. We need to get to the roots of our pain. I have talked to so many survivors that get stuck here and never see the gates of healing.

Self-examination will be the most difficult at the start, but once you get going on it, I think it gets easier. The hardest part will be the initial realization that some things you have done might be because of your past and then you beat yourself up and get angry at yourself. This is one reason that I suggest a good therapist to help you through this. Recognize the rotten apples, then be kind to yourself and forgive yourself! All survivors usually make negative decisions based on their particular trauma, you are not alone, get through it, and then move on to the gates. Because this particular station in the corridors of healing can be so difficult, you need something to help you along.

That "something" is in the form of gratitude. Believe me (because I have gone through this), finding things to be grateful for makes this particular exercise so much easier!

I believe that gratitude, for most of us, does not come naturally, we need to develop it. Unlike picking out the rotten squishy apples of our past, gratitude is pleasant and can be relatively easy, we just need to make it a habit. If a grateful, thankful heart came easy to us, the advertising agencies would be out of business. It is no secret that marketing products and services in creative ways increases sales volume. If the message of the sales hype is "You are just no good without this," and we believe it, then the sales are better. When do you ever see marketing media encouraging gratitude? Gratitude does not sell stuff. If we are grateful, we might not think we need what is offered.

We always seem to want more, need more, and improve on our stuff. I personally enjoy "stuff." I like how it makes me feel! The feeling may be temporary, but I like it! I like a luxury car, nice clothes, home decorations, vacations, and I really love my cell phone! We all like stuff!

As a human being and citizen of the United States, I feel entitled to good roads and safe bridges, fire and police protection, and scores of other things I take for granted because I pay taxes.

I think that, as a society, we may be so busy feeling entitled, that we have lost the wonder of the world we live in!

As a trauma survivor, I have sometimes been so engrossed with the issues of the past that I have lost the joy of the present. I have learned that if I consciously focus on the joys of the present, with gratitude, that my past is not as big of an issue.

The conclusion to these thoughts is this: an attitude of gratitude helps me heal and increases my happiness.

I know this may sound too simple to some people, and many will be tempted to just skip over this step, but it actually is more important than you think. Because I was born in the United States, I think I have lost the "wonder" of many things. It has been my mission to try and recapture that wonder.

Next time you go out to a buffet dinner, take the time to marvel at all the sights and sounds and smells around you. There are others in this world that do not have this privilege. Think about everything around you and live in the present as if you are looking at the colors of the food for the first time. Pretend that this is the first time you have ever looked upon or smelled something so heavenly.

When you really look and focus on these small things, you will appreciate them more. If this simple exercise seems silly to you, then close your eyes and take a few minutes to imagine all of this gone forever. God has provided all of this for us, we need to thank Him.

Expand your focus of gratitude for the rest of your day and your whole outlook will probably be different. As you climb into your automobile, even if it is quite rusty, remember that at one time this would be a thing that everyone would have marveled at, if they had never seen or owned one.

Your trauma was designed by the evil one to make you fear, dread, and hate each day. Do not let evil win. Learn to focus on the positive things and crowd out the negative. Do not let evil win, don't give into it.

Focus on the here and now and marvel at the sunsets, flowers, healthy children, and blessings in your life. If your blessings are monster trucks, tropical vacations, a good spouse, new carpet, or any other thing in your life, thank Father God for them. He has provided all these things for our blessing and enjoyment.

Action Plan and Assignment

1. Take yourself out to eat at a great buffet and marvel at all the sights, smells, and sounds.

2. Write down the ways you think that the past might have affected your life, including your present day.

3. Read Psalm 92 and Psalm 150.

4. Identify and write down each fear. Pray over each one, giving and surrendering each fear to God. Name each fear again and ask Him to deliver you.

5. Most importantly, take time to be thankful for the gift of Jesus Christ who has paid for your sins.

16

You Have Power

All of us who have been traumatized have had the feeling of being powerless. I do not believe that there are adequate words to describe the helpless, powerless panic we felt when we were in the middle of someone else's selfish act of sadism toward us.

I have vowed to myself that I will never be powerless again. I took self-defense classes. I lock doors. I check doors I have already locked. I scan parking lots when walking to and from my car. I am aware of my surroundings. I live by the creed, "You have to earn my trust." I park under lights. I put security freeze on my credit. I lock my car and request a cruiser if I have a breakdown. I allow my dog to intimidate strangers who come to my house. I limit personal information that I give out. I avoid people who trigger me (funny how I can always sense a pedophile, even if no one tells me). I keep my phone with me at all times. I pay attention and pay attention and pay attention. Most importantly, I pray and I praise God. I think that prayer is the one over all thing that gives us power. Long ago, I used to be somewhat ambivalent about prayer. I would think that, if God already knows everything, then why bother him with stuff he already knows? Doesn't he have better things to do with his time than hear me talk about things he already knows?

I was reading the Bible one day and had a new revelation. Well, it was new to me anyway. I was reading Ezekiel 37:1–10.

As I read this passage, I finally got the message. The message is this: there is power in my words. Months before this, as I studied the word of God, I learned that prayer, just for the sake of prayer, pleases God and is comforting for me, but this time, I learned something that I had not heard much teaching or preaching about. I learned that there is unbelievable power in our words.

In the passages, when Ezekiel spoke to the bones (as God told him to), they became living flesh. When he spoke to the wind, it obeyed.

Now, I am not going to tell you to speak to the dead and you will raise them because in the scriptural passage the predominant message was that the dead bones represented Israel. But in these passages I believe that the word of God can also teach us something else. The fact that our words are powerful is the big lesson we can take away here. God could have spoken to the bones himself and they would have risen.

God instructed Ezekiel to speak to the bones to show us that our words have more merit than we give them credit.

I knew that God was showing Ezekiel many things in this passage of scripture, but what I came away with was a new thought for either saying or controlling the words that pop into my head. I need to be more careful because there is power in my speech.

If there is truly power in my speech, then prayer is more powerful than I had ever dreamed. I decided then and there that going very long without talking to God was not in my best interest.

From that moment on, I have determined to be very careful of what comes out of my mouth. I am not going to lie to you and tell you that I am 100 percent successful in this quest, but I am getting better and trying harder all the time.

Proverbs 18: 21 tells us that "death and life are in the power of the tongue." If you do not believe this, think back to a time when someone hurt you deeply with their tongue. Don't dwell on the incident, just acknowledge it.

Proverbs 10: 20 says that the tongue of the just is as choice silver.

Proverbs 15:4 says that a wholesome tongue is a tree of life.

Proverbs 21: 23 says that whoso keepeth his tongue, keepeth his soul.

Proverbs 25:15 says that a soft tongue breaks the bone.

Jeremiah 18: 18 says let us smite him with the tongue.

James 1: 6 says that the tongue is a fire.

I do not think we can really state just how much our speech affects all those around us, never mind ourselves. We can easily tear down or build up and edify another human being, but we can just as easily hurt or edify God with our words. Our words to God are always heard and understood. He wants to hear us and even Jesus was our example, instructing us to pray and setting the example for us.

We can ask for peace, safety, understanding, and healing as well as all the personal things we desire. Thank Him in advance for the answers.

Through the years, I have found that sometimes my prayers are answered in the way I want, right away. Sometimes, I have had to wait a while (sometimes a long while) for a positive answer. Sometimes, the answer has been "no." When the answer was no, I always have found out later that it was the best thing for me because God had something better.

Remember this as you pray through, it is always the will of God to give you the emotional healing you desire. When you seek and ask for healing, He will always hear you.

God already knows what we want before we ask, but I think of prayer like I think of electricity. I need to turn the electricity on.

If the room is dark, I switch on the light if I want light. The power is already there, but I have to activate it.

By an action of faith in the light switch, I turn on the light to activate its power to illuminate the room.

Our action of faith is prayer. Prayer is the "switch" that activates the requests you have, requests and needs He already knows. God has loved us so much that He has given us this infinite kind of power through prayer!

Jesus said that we have not because we ask not. I prefer to ask. When I pray, I feel powerful over all the evil things and people. God's light is greater than evil's darkness. Darkness abducted me once, but now I can bathe my life in God's light! If you had been with me in the torture room and heard the things they chanted and said, you would know firsthand like I do, how much evil really hates light and prayer to God. Evil hates prayer because prayer is power. When I pray, I feel powerful and loved because I know He is listening, and He loves me.

Let me encourage you to take back the power of your emotional life through prayer, several times a day.

You can pray anytime anywhere, there is no set posture, time, or place. He hears you wherever you are. Prayer is God and I having a chat.

Mark 11: 22 says that whosoever (that includes you and me) shall say to this mountain (trauma is a mountain) be thou removed and be cast into the sea and shall not doubt in his heart but shall believe that those things which he saith shall come to pass; he shall have whatsoever he saith.

If you want to change your life, make a different choice.

Action Plan and Assignment

1. Accept the fact that your speech and prayers are powerful.
2. Read Mark 11:22–26.
3. Read 2 Thessalonains 3:1 and 2.
4. Read Luke 11: 9 and 10.
5. Read Ezekiel 37:1–10.
6. Read Romans 14:11.

17

Shake, Rattle, and Roll

Shake, rattle, and roll is the description of sleep for many people. PTSD and various traumas might keep us from sleep. I am happy to say that shake, rattle, and roll is not a typical description of my sleep habits these days. I only have night terrors occasionally, once a year at most, and this is usually brought on by multiple triggers in my day and evening. Lack of sleep can sometimes be caused by fear and a lack of trust in God. The trust part was very difficult for me. I kept wondering how I could feel safe and trust God today when I certainly did not feel protected at five years old. Then I wondered, maybe He did protect me, after all, I did not die.

Then I thought, *Big deal! Why could He not just keep me from the trauma? Why did He let it happen? If He did not stop these vile people then, how can I trust him now?*

This, for me, was the most difficult part of my healing. I struggled with this so often that this subject also caused many sleepless nights. I went back to my therapist and asked for help. No answers there. I discussed my problem with clergy, but somehow, I couldn't grasp a peaceful truth there either. They were probably telling me exactly what I finally figured out; maybe I just was not listening closely enough.

As I inched my way through the corridors, I actually stayed at this station for quite some time, delaying my progression to the healing gates, feeling jumpy, frightful, and miserable.

While reading Psalms one day, I think I figured it out. I was reading Psalm 37. Psalm 37 is probably my all-time favorite

Psalm. The Psalm starts out by talking about "evildoers." I really liked that and could identify with the words easily. The words gave me peace because my abusers were never brought to justice in this life.

As I reread the Psalm, I came to the last verse again and I finally understood trust. I finally came to terms about what trust really is. "And the Lord shall help them and deliver them: he shall deliver them from the wicked and save them because (watch this) they trust in him" (Psalm 37:40).

Bad things can happen to all of us. God is not responsible for the evil choices of people. We all make our own choices. That is not a reason to withhold our trust in Him. I then understood why trust was so difficult for me. I was approaching the subject of trust and treating it like a feeling.

Trust is not a feeling; trust is an act of obedience. Obey God by trusting in Him, and according to Psalm 37:40, "He will deliver and save me from the wicked." I saw that the scripture did not say that I would never suffer under the selfish hand of someone who hates God, it just says everything will be okay. In one way or another, He will deliver me and everything will be okay. Pain and suffering happens, but it is temporary.

I think this point needs to be highlighted and committed to memory, the point of truth is that, pain and suffering happens, but it is temporary, and I prolong the pain and suffering by not trusting God and refusing to move beyond the trauma.

God needs me to trust Him, and I need me to trust Him too. These are two sides to the same coin. Trusting God is good for me and makes my life easier. I do know that I have already covered the subject of trust in chapter 3, titled "Close Your Eyes," but we who are survivors have problems with this concept again and again throughout our lives, and it needs to be repeatedly addressed.

We need to declare trust once and for all at an early point in our healing, then we need to revisit our decision occasionally. This is about that time of revisiting. And I need to add here that although I have walked through the healing gates, there are times even now that I need to remind myself that trusting God is my best option and choice.

By an act of my will, I decided to trust the holy living God of the universe. I decided to trust the God that sent Jesus Christ to earth to die and sacrifice for the payment of my sins.

I again thought of Jesus. God did not send angels to take him off the cross and ease his suffering. Christ suffered. Jesus was mocked, beaten, scorned, and even abandoned by his friends in his hour of greatest need.

Did God intervene in any of that?

No, God did not intervene and cause all the soldiers that mocked him to get laryngitis. God did not place obstacles in the way of those who were beating him, and the nails were real nails, not movie props. Jesus suffered embarrassment and shame, and God did not stop the evil from happening. Still, Jesus trusted the heavenly Father. Jesus trusted God that from his suffering, a greater good would come. Jesus suffered the punishment that mankind deserved. He did not deserve to suffer, but we all do, because none of us is sinless and pure like Jesus. Because of his gift if His life, I can be free of the torment of hell that God prepared for the devil and his angels. All I have to do is accept it. All I have to do is accept His gift and repent of my sin, and then I am "plugged in" to the love of God.

When I looked at my suffering in the light of the suffering of Jesus, my whole attitude changed. I wanted to obey and I wanted to trust Him.

From that moment on, I knew that everything would be okay. No matter what storms I might weather, what betrayals I might endure, what sickness I might feel, everything would be okay, but sometimes, I still had to remind myself of my choice to trust. I may not ever feel pain again, but if I do, I know I can trust Him, it is all okay. Habakkuk 3:17 and 18 became my mantra. These scriptures are in your action plan. Be sure to read them!

This life, after all, is but for a moment. Eternity is a long time. I chose not to disobey God in my temporary life so that I could have more joy in my eternal life. As I progressed farther and farther through my journey to the gates of healing, it was clear and apparent to me that healing is actually a series of choices we make. I could more clearly see that my fellow sufferers were usually "stuck" at one or more of the stations of healing, desperately suffering, being in pain, but insisting that the choices that could give them victory were impossible for them to do.

The phrase "I can't" is readily on the lips of so many survivors because they choose not to have the courage to do the difficult things, such as trusting in God, in spite of the trauma they suffered.

Trusting God when the field is full of flowers, the bank account is fat, and our bellies are full is easy. I do not believe that too many of us (maybe none of us) will get rewards in heaven because we trusted God when our circumstances were rosy. I believe that the scriptures teach us that, there will be great rewards for those of us who continue to trust God when our circumstances have been horrible and our futures seem uncertain.

I know it was at this particular point of my healing that I knew beyond a shadow of doubt that healing is really a choice. I determined to take the combination of words that form that horrible phrase "I can't" out of my vocabulary and do the choices necessary to heal.

After my life-changing decision to trust Him, the Lord reminded me of a few things in my past that my anger and mistrust had masked.

I was born in the 1950s, over two months premature. In the 1950s, this was very serious. At that time, there did not exist the sophisticated instruments and knowledge that we have today that give a preemie a better start. The infant mortality was much higher than it is today, and a premature birth would most likely ensure a life of physical problems and innumerable difficulties, that is if the baby survived.

It is a miracle that I was born at all. Because of other complications, my mother and I both came very close to death that day.

I have suffered no ill effects from the premature birth even without the benefit of twenty-first century knowledge. I always marvel when I hear or read about the inevitable difficulties that seven-month babies will face in their future, because not only have I none of these problems, but I am blessed with a relatively high IQ, which I have been informed is almost impossible for a child with my start in life. Clearly, my heavenly Father has intervened in this situation.

I was not quite two when I contracted German measles. From my mother's accounts of that time, I think I may not have been expected to survive that either, especially without some permanent damage, but I have no ill effects of the disease today. God had intervened early in my life, and He had been watching over me. He was aware of the day that I was abducted. He did not let them take my life, even though at one point I really thought I was going to die. Satan worshipers have ways of getting rid of bodies without leaving a trace. It happens every day, all over the world.

As I pondered and thought over all the details of these things, and so much more, I realized that, I truly am a better person for all I have suffered. I decided to work out how I could make all my negative experiences count for good. I realized that my sufferings do not define me, they are merely chapters in my life. If I do not make the necessary choices I need to heal, my sufferings can easily define me.

I have lived long enough to meet some people who have lived what we can define as a "charmed life." It seems that the worst suffering they have felt is a hangnail in primary school and a fender bender in the mall parking lot. There was always plenty of money, and if difficulty arose, their parents would bail them out, so they did not have to feel the consequences of the actions of others, much less their own.

As adults, they seem practically useless. I know that there are exceptions, but the general rule is that if we deal with negative things in a proper spiritual attitude, we can become people of exceptional character. When all of life has been wonderful, the means to build spiritual muscle and great character seems to be lost. What is that saying? "No gain without pain?" I think it applies to more than just physical discomfort in the gym.

I have told my children, over and over, as they were growing up, that the only thing you will take into eternity is the character you build here on earth. Character, goodness, and love are the only things that can survive the transition from our mortal bodies to our spiritual beings.

The only things that we will take into eternity is the character we develop here on earth.

I think the above truth puts a whole new perspective on the subject of trauma and the trusting of God. What happened to me does not matter nearly as much as what I do with it. I can let my trauma destroy me, or I can use it as a tool to help me choose the good ways of life. I can choose to trust God and build upon the experience, things like unselfishness, faith, honesty, integrity, and peace. If everything in my life had been wonderful, I would not have the opportunity to have these rewards given to me by a gracious Father, when someday I get to see Him, face-to-face.

No one gets rewards for things that are not a challenge. Only challenging activities get the trophy and the prize. The world does not give out rewards to people who have not overcome challenges. Trophies and prizes and glory do not go to those who are at the starting gate thinking about running the race. These people are forgotten as the attention is showered on the winner, who has put forth the effort, endured the discomfort, and finished the race. I do not think God gives the glory to the starters and thinkers either. I think he mainly rewards the efforts of those of us who have overcome incredible odds.

For the first time in my life, I thanked God for the abduction. I would rather have a time of discomfort if I can have an opportunity for greater things. I would rather suffer some pain and learn to be strong than to have had a charmed life and be weak.

I raise chickens. When a baby chick is born, it struggles terribly when getting out of its shell. So often I have been tempted to ask someone to tie my hands behind my back during this time. It is so difficult for me to not just help the chick along, but I know that if I break the shell for the chick and help it on its way, that it will be a weak chicken and probably not even get to adulthood.

Suffering can be a prosperous part of growing and living, the choice is ours. Because we can do something positive with our suffering does not mean that God is pleased with the perpetrators of our trauma. The Bible teaches us that He hates wickedness and sin. The Word of God teaches that He will punish the wicked, but suffering can be transformed into a beautiful life if we trust Him. The best illustration of this point can be found in a story in the book of Genesis. The true story of Joseph is an inspiration to all who will hear it. Joseph was one of twelve children, hated by his brothers, who were intensely jealous of him. The brothers plotted together, then sold Joseph into slavery, and concocted a lie, telling their father that wild animals had killed him.

The way Joseph handled this entire trauma and pain is an inspiration to us all. The complete story of how Joseph turned a bad time into blessings for his whole family is part of your action plan. Do take time to read all of the story, I think it will give you a lift.

The decision to trust God came with a decision to stop letting fear rule my life. Yes, I do get fearful at times, but I always refer back to the scripture references on fear and remind myself that I made a choice not to let fear rule my life. I am quickly brought back to the spiritual balance I need to be. Anxiety and triggers will come sometimes to annoy me, but fear is not my lifestyle, there is a big difference.

I can be careful and take precautions to keep myself safe (God expects us to have common sense), but I do not have to daily tremble, worry, and lose sleep. In other words, I may have to deal with a fearful situation sometimes, but I can choose not to let fear run my life, ruin every day of my life, and suffer with needless anxiety

I found Isaiah 51:7 to be helpful, it says:

> Fear not the reproach of men, neither be afraid of their revilings.
>
> I even I am he that comforteth you; who art thou, that thou shouldest be afraid of a man that shall die, and the son of man which shall be made as grass; And forgettest the Lord thy maker, that hath stretch forth the heavens and laid the foundations of the earth; and hast feared continually every day because of the fury of the oppressor, as if he were ready to destroy? And where is the fury of the oppressor? (Isaiah 51:12, 13)

In conclusion, God has given me the gift of fear to deal with an immediate situation that may require me to protect myself, such as watching someone come into a bank with a gun. My fear tells me to leave. My fear can protect me in some life situations.

If the incident has passed, such as my childhood trauma, fear can keep me from living my life. When I choose to trust God, I do not fear so much. Trust is something I consciously decide to do every day. Learning to trust God is one of the major stops you need to make as you go through the corridors, then onto the gates of freedom.

Our enemy, the devil, is constantly trying to give us reasons not to trust God. As I choose to obey and trust God, the devil gets irritated and moves on.

Trust is an exercise I choose to do each day, and the days I forget are usually pretty tough days!

Action Plan and Assignment

1. Read Habakkuk 3:17, 18.

2. Read Psalm 37.

3. Read the account of Joseph in Genesis chapters 39–45 and rejoice with Joseph as all of the bad things done to him in his life are turned around for the good of all.

4. Choose to trust God, just like Habakkuk did.

18

Managing Night Terrors

Probably every person in the world experiences nightmares sometimes. For those of us who have been traumatized, nightmares take on a whole new level. People whose most traumatic experience in life was a scratch on their new car will not really understand this. The same goes for people who have had troubles but not severe personal trauma, they just cannot understand night terrors. It is like trying to explain to someone what water feels like. They understand "wet" but how do you really describe "wet?" It is what it is!

If you have been diagnosed PTSD, you fully understand the dynamics of night terrors and have the frustration of being unable to control so much of them. I think that in all my years of therapy and counseling, how to handle night terrors was never addressed.

The normal person may have a nightmare, wake up, thank God that it was only a dream, and go back to sleep. Not so with us trauma survivors. There are no real words in any language that sufficiently describe night terror flashbacks.

In the dream, persons and places might be the same or they may be a bit different, but the injury and experience is always the same. You are there again. You are experiencing your undeserved trauma all over again. All the feelings, colors, fear, injustices, and hell, you are reliving. You are there. When you wake up, you do not shake it off and go back to sleep. You are exhausted, frustrated, fearful, angry, and physically in pain.

I do not experience night terrors very often now, no more than once a year usually. Most of the time, if I have a nightmare, it is the same annoying experience that most people encounter, meaning that the dream is weird, but just a dream and I go back to sleep.

When I do experience a flashback night terror, the theme is always the same. I am trapped. I cannot get to safety. There are evil people trying to control me. I try the doors, I escape for a few steps and get caught by the evil people. I try more ways to escape. Nothing budges, no doors work. There are no windows. No one can hear me scream. I try to scream, but no sound emerges from my mouth. I sweat profusely. I feel intense fear. I hear the evil people talk and they try to convince me that if I let them control me, all will be well. I hear them lie and tell me they will not hurt me. I run, I try more doors, I panic. I find another avenue that may lead to safety. I get caught. I wake up.

I feel afraid, mentally exhausted, traumatized, and cannot go back to sleep. I reason it out, telling myself that it was only a dream and I am now safe. I say some prayers.

I get up and go to the bathroom, drink some water, and try to shake it off. I am cold and my whole body hurts. My jaws hurt the worst as I have been clenching my teeth in my sleep. The pain radiates from my jaws to my whole head. I take pain medicine. I drink more water and again try to shake it off. I shudder a bit and feel very nauseated. Then I get even colder, stumble back to bed, and try to sleep again, but sleep does not come. I assume that most people reading this can identify with my night terror scenario. The details of your nightmares will probably be different, but the physical and emotional feelings are the same. You are reliving your trauma. Your head is replaying your worst nightmare, and unfortunately, this nightmare was at one time real. You are reliving it. If you do not find a constructive way to deal with your night terror, your whole next day is ruined. The best way I have found to deal with night terror is to get out of bed and do something to get my mind out of the dump. If you like to read, reading is a good option, preferably something light and funny. I would not consider the Bible to be "light and funny," but reading it at this time gives comfort and helps me to "center" myself emotionally. Sometimes, I have gone out into my studio and worked on a sewing project. Sometimes, TV is a good way to unsettle myself. If you are overweight, snacking at this time could be disastrous to your diet, but if you do decide to snack, milk is a good choice. The calcium in dairy products, such as milk, ice cream, yogurt, or pudding, can have a natural calming effect on humans.

Have you ever seen new babies that do not sleep after they have their milk? New babies are on a diet of total milk and they sleep most of the time. Milk (unless you are allergic to it) contains agents that are naturally calming and sometimes sleep inducing if you have enough. A big bowl of macaroni and cheese will almost put me into a coma! Oats and turkey can induce calm in many people. I keep a bottle of an herbal calming solution next to my bedside for these little "emergencies" and it helps. Some herbs act as mild sedatives, but I will not tell you which ones do, for a very good reason. Before you go to the vitamin store and make a purchase of an herbal sedative, talk to your doctor. Let your doctor know of which herbs you are considering. Herbs are medicines and need to be treated as such. Some herbs have a negative effect if taken with other herbs and some can interfere with prescribed medications you are taking. Check with your doctor before you self-medicate. What works for me may be disastrous for you! I think that avoiding the triggers that can bring on the night terrors is a good plan of action. This, again, is something that you may want to discuss with your therapist. Relate the dream and brainstorm with him/her about what may have triggered the dream, then try to avoid the people, places, or things. Some things may be difficult or almost impossible for you to avoid, this is where God comes into view. Praise Him, then ask Him to deliver you from this problem. This will come under the category of God doing for you what you cannot do for yourself.

For me, constant night terrors were like the chains falling off Peter's hands. God got rid of it for me because I could not do it for myself. Night terrors can be difficult to manage so do not be afraid to talk to your doctor about them, but be warned that, in my opinion, some medications will bring on night terrors. For me, all sleep-inducing medications will bring on severe nightmares, so I avoid them. This may not be the case for you. Again, work with your doctor and find the solutions that are best for you. What encourages a night terror in me may be restful for you! But always praise and pray for deliverance! The goal here is to stop reliving the trauma you experienced. If I am spending time with a person who has a severely controlling personality, I can quite often expect nightmares. I have gone to great lengths to avoid these kinds of people. A controller or manipulator can give me anxiety when I am with them and a real bad dream later. I just avoid them and I never call them my friend. I just pray for them. What you need to avoid or curtail may be different from what I need to do, but love yourself enough to do it anyway! Avoid your triggers to have better sleep. I know that sometimes night terrors come on without triggers, keep asking for deliverance. God hears our prayers.

Above all, I have learned that praise to the one true God, the ancient of days helps me more than anything. Then, as long as I am fully awake, Bible reading or any other of the abovementioned activities completely gets my mind off the night terror and I again am calm.

Putting your earbuds in and putting on some praise or other soothing music can help also, and if you sing along with the music, I guess you are truly singing in the night.

Action Plan and Assignment

1. Read Psalm 91 every night before bed.
2. Read Psalm 4:8, it will comfort you.

19

Choose What You Think

Whatsoever things are true, whatsoever things are honest, whatsoever things are just, whatsoever things are pure, whatsoever things are lovely, whatsoever things are of good report; if there be any virtue, and if there be any praise, think on these things. (Philippians 4:8)

I must admit that for many years of my Christian life, I did not pay much attention to this passage of scripture or even take it too seriously, but God does not have anything in his word that does not have a purpose. Nothing is put in the Bible to take up space or just to sound pretty. All scripture should be taken seriously, even Philippians 4:8.

As I was searching the scripture for coping mechanisms that may lead to emotional healing, I came across this passage. I guess I never thought this passage was very important, probably because I had never heard a sermon on it. I suppose somewhere, sometime, there has been a sermon preached on these verses, but I had never heard one. I surmised that this may be something that is not popular to speak on from the pulpit, just like the scripture that tells men to love their wives as Christ loved the church and gave himself for it. In over thirty years, no minister that I have ever met wants to tackle that subject! I think if messengers of God would boldly preach on this, the Christian divorce rate would fall considerably.

Well, I will get off my soap box now and get back to the subject at hand. I read the verses in Philippians 4:8 with new eyes, and for the first time in my life, I realized that these are not just nice flowery words but direct commands from God. Paul says in 2 Corinthians 10:5 to bring every thought into captivity. That always made sense to me. Do not allow myself to dwell on negative or unclean thoughts. I get that. But purposely being commanded to think nice things, that was a new concept for me. I decided that I would deliberately make my thoughts pleasing and honest and true and pure.

As the days progressed to weeks and then months, I began to notice that going through the corridors and progressing through to the iron gates seemed easier. Why was it easier? What had changed? My circumstances had not changed. My memories of abuse had not faded. I began to notice that my flashbacks were fewer and my days were easier. So what was different? Had I changed? Was God doing a miracle? I do believe in miracles, but I came to the conclusion that this was not one of them, unless you believe that miracles automatically come out of obedience, I pondered these things. I now know that the reason that my progression through the corridors was easier was far simpler. I was thinking differently. My circumstances were not changing, but I was. I was thinking differently and nice thoughts were the lights guiding me to the gates of freedom. When the dark darts of Satan's arsenal come at you, it is easy to remain focused on the damage. Usually, your damage control plan regularly comes in the form of deciding not to dwell on or think about the trauma.

Everyone knows that if you are determined not to think about something, that is *all* you will think about. If you tell yourself that you will not think about your trauma, your trauma will be in your thoughts always and it can lead to anger and depression and despair.

I learned that if I wanted to stop thinking about the negative, I should do just the opposite. I should think about positive things, just like the scripture says. Such a simple concept, easy to do, yet with profound results! I have met some people who are constantly upbeat and always have a positive attitude. These kinds of people smile often, complain little, and seem to breeze through life easier even when they are faced with challenges.

I have wondered, are they born this way? Is a positive cheerful countenance a specific personality that they are born with? Is there such a thing as a gene of optimism written on the DNA of some people?

If there is such a thing as a positive cheerful gene, I was not blessed with one. I have to work at it. Negative junk comes easy, focus on the good requires intent. Philippians 4:8 tells us exactly how to achieve a positive attitude. It says to speak to ourselves in songs of praise and worship. I have developed a new habit that I think could benefit everyone. Instead of flipping on the news programs every morning, I read the Bible, starting with a Psalm of praise. My favorites are Psalms 148, 149, and 150. I read the selected Psalm out loud and focus on each word. I cannot fully express how profoundly this little exercise has changed my life. My whole outlook on the day is brighter, and I seem to be more spiritual. Mark has recently joined me in the morning ritual and he also thinks his days are better. After the Psalm, we read other passages of scripture and pray. Focus on God first thing in the morning can put all sorts of problems and tiresome duties into perspective. If you determine to keep your focus on the Lord all day, some problems just melt away. Praising and singing about our Lord always chases away the demonic influences that enjoy ruining our days. Mark injured his knee quite recently. He was in some serious pain, walking with a cane, and on pain medication. If Mark takes pain meds, it is a big deal indeed, as he has one of the highest pain tolerances of anyone I have ever known.

On a recent Sunday, we started our morning with our Bible reading and prayer even though Mark was not feeling well. Some days Mark will read, other days I read the Word out loud and we can talk about it together. This was a typical Sunday morning in that we had our devotional time, enjoyed breakfast together, and headed for church. I wondered about Mark actually going as he was leaning heavily on his cane, but he managed.

After church fellowship, one of the men suggested prayer for Mark. The whole congregation of our little church asked God to heal Mark. He says he felt a strange warm sensation come over his body that he had never felt before.

My husband walked out of the church that morning without his cane. Mark's knee was healed. He climbed into the ranch truck the next morning without his cane and minus his limp. The omission of his knee brace let me know that God had truly given us a miracle and a blessing.

There are two things here that are interesting to note:

1. Miracles like this never happened to us until we started that morning praise ritual together, and

2. I realized that emotional healing can possibly come the same way, but I think that praise is necessary.

I think that immediate miraculous emotional healing is rare because trauma damages so many areas of our thinking, emotions, and decisions. Not impossible, but rare because there are so many negative things we choose to hold on to that can be traced to our past negative history. It is the negative things we choose to hold on to that interfere with God's plan to heal us.

I believe that trauma damages us in so many layers, that each layer has to be peeled back, examined, and ultimately discarded. I know from experience that praise to our God can shorten this process and provide healing to each layer. If you are serious about healing and moving on with your life, you cannot skip this step. You must make it a habit and love God more for it, then begin to experience faster healing. I was not there, but I would be willing to bet my life that when the angel was leading Peter out of the prison, that Peter was not grumbling, but praising God, even if it was silent to everyone else. The Bible tells us that when Paul was in prison, he praised and sang songs to God, and I think we should do the same, even when we do not feel like it. Progressing through the corridors to the iron gates does not require weapons like swords, guns, or even hand-to-hand combat. Peter did not encounter a single person to fight with while he stepped closer and closer to the gates of freedom. God provided what Peter could not do, in this case no human opposition, Peter did what he could do, which was, keep on walking. Long after the abuse, trauma, neglect, and indignities have passed, they live on in the mind and heart of the survivor. This is where the real battle is. This is the battle that few will ever glimpse and only the survivor and God will ever really see. These memories become our worst enemies, and since the memories reside in our minds, we can become our own worst enemy.

The offense or offenses may be long past, but the fight in our minds intensifies all of the anger, hate, confusion, and fear. Usually, we are walking or even running through the dark corridors of the prison, fighting our minds through to the iron gates, forgetting the principles in the Word of God that were provided there to make the journey easier.

Think of Philippians 4: 8 as "whistling past the graveyard." Sometimes, when people are afraid of things or situations, they whistle or sing. Some people whistle or sing when they pass a cemetery because they are truly afraid of the dead. Whistling calms their nerves and puts their minds in a different place. God has provided this same concept for us to help us. When we are focusing on whatsoever things are true and whatsoever things are lovely, we put ourselves into a different place.

I am not saying to deny the atrocities that happened to you, I am not saying to be in denial. Most people need to go over those incidents with a qualified professional. Denial is not a healthy option for anyone. What I am saying is, sometimes we have to whistle past the graveyard. The challenges of life itself can be a frightening cemetery. Beginning the day with Bible verses, coupled with praise and worship, even if for only a few minutes is a practical way to "whistle past the graveyard" and heal faster.

When we focus and think on the things that are true, just, pure, lovely, and of good report, we give our minds a rest. The truest, purest, loveliest things in the world are found in God's word.

No general can send his men into battle twenty-four hours a day, seven days a week. The soldiers could never keep up that pace, they need rest and so do we. We who have known trauma are going through a dark prison doing great battles in our minds. This can get really exhausting and we might be tempted to just sit down and give up before we get to the gates.

Training the mind to think on nice things is a great tool. You can start by praise to God, but you do not have to focus on praise twenty-four hours a day, and I do not believe God expects us to. Are you interested in fishing, baseball, skiing, running, or some other sport? Think about that more often.

After you praise God, consciously think about your children, your club, your vacation, your hobbies, or anything that is pleasant as soon as the past tries to bite you in the behind.

I have been an avid quilter for over thirty-seven years. Colors and shapes make me happy. I would much rather think about colors and shapes than negative images. Imagine yourself not only getting a hole in one, but having countless people around to see it!

Notice pretty sunsets, your garden, your pets, or anything that boosts your spirits and makes you happy. And remember, you are commanded to do this by God himself! What a great God we serve!

In Isaiah 61:3, I read about "putting on a garment of praise." I believe this is a poetic way to say that we should praise God and do it regularly. Thank Him constantly for all his blessings.

Yes, some of us have been traumatized, but if we take the focus off that for a while and thank him for all the good things in life, we will feel better. Focus on the pleasant things in life and praising

God may not take away the consequences of the atrocities, but it will make it easier to live with. I am not a scientist, but for me, praising seems to raise my serotonin level and all those other brain chemicals that make me feel good.

If you need an even extra boost in the "feeling better" department, physical exercise in conjunction with practicing good thoughts is a great way to defeat the enemy and have a good life.

> Those things which we have both learned and received and heard and seen in me do: and the God of peace shall be with you. (Philippians 4:9)

Action Plan and Assignment

1. Read 2 Corinthians 10:4 and 5.

2. Start every day with praise and Bible reading; suggestions are Psalms 148, 149, and 150.

3. 3. Determine to live Philippians 4: 8.

4. Read Ephesians 5:19.

20

Anger Is a Choice

I stopped going to group therapy less than a year after I started group therapy. This was the day that I asked every lady how long she had been in therapy and was very disappointed with the answers.

What I observed was that although each woman told me that she had been in therapy for five to twenty years, no one was any further in her therapy than I was, and I had just started! Everyone in my therapy group for abused women was right there where I was, stuck in angry. Each lady was struggling with all the same issues that I was, and none of them had found relief or answers for any of the issues that I have talked about in my previous chapters. Of all the issues I was struggling with, anger was the number 1 subject that I really wanted to heal. I did not wish to stay angry for the rest of my life. Anger takes too much energy and robs me of precious moments in my life. Instead of enjoying my family, I would be angry with my abductors. Instead of enjoying my dinner, I would be fantasizing about how they could experience the same treatment they gave me. I would replay all the struggles I have experienced in life that directly relate to my childhood, then be angry at my church because "the biggest church in the county" did not take seriously the pain of a woman who was still living out the past. I used to wish I would get cancer, they would rally round me and give support then, but a woman struggling with great emotional trauma, they shoved aside. I was angry. Why could they not open the Bible and tell me how to heal? How could they not know? They were the ones that went to seminary! Didn't seminary teach about healing? I was angry. I reasoned that they were the ones who went to seminary, so they know more than I do; the advice given was not working, so there must be something wrong with me! It must be me, not them. I was angry. Instead of marveling at the sunshine and the plants in my vegetable garden, I was angrily focused on what the abduction had cost me, the insensitivity of some people who mocked and enjoyed my misery (while calling themselves Christians of course) and on and on and on. I had an abundance of offenses to be angry about and ultimately was angry at God for not stopping all of those nasty people from hurting me. I had not yet found the story of Peter in prison. I had not even begun to get onto my feet, let alone walk through the corridors. Anger was eating me from the inside out, affecting me emotionally, physically, and spiritually. When I observed that ladies who had been in therapy were stuck on the same treadmill that I was, my anger gave way to panic and I began to look for a solution to the destructive path I was on. I even contemplated suicide as an option.

Even though I had not found Peter in prison yet (I had read the scripture but never really got the message), I began to see that I had a choice. I could stay angry and let it poison my whole life, or I could let it go. How could I let it go? Do I just forgive those that negatively influenced my life, but those around me as well? How dare they do such vile things to me *and* to other children and families and just live their lives unaffected! How could that be fair? I knew that I was not the only victim, their whole chamber was set up specifically for children.

I remember telling my therapist details that no one else will ever hear, then begging her to tell me that all this is totally absurd. I wished for her to tell me that I must have had bad dreams, a product of a hyper imagination, tell me I made it up, give me some pills, and let me sink into a blissful state of denial! Pretending that the trauma did not exist seemed far easier than dealing with the anger, hate, pain, and loss.

I was disappointed when she told me that I was indeed abused in the ways I remembered because she had heard all the details before. My description of the room, child's coffin, blood, and everything else was identical to stories she had heard from others. Stories of other people I had never met. I knew that I had never read or heard about these details of horror, I had always kept my distance from stories or images of anything traumatic.

The thought of really having to deal with all the garbage was overwhelming. I felt a fresh new burst of anger. I did not want to look at it again and face facts, I just would rather be dead. I prayed for Jesus to grant me some kind of terminal disease so that I could just go home and see Him and all this pain would be gone. My doctor put me on medication and I faced my therapist one more time.

I felt even more frustrated knowing that groups of other ritual survivors would not accept me into their group because I was not MPD (multiple personality disorder). I became angry at law enforcement and the judicial system, more anger to deal with. How could I not be angry at them, after all, how often do you hear of people engaged in ritual abuse being prosecuted? Some people say that what happened to me does not exist because if it did, the law would do something about it. I was angry at all of them too. How dare society and our judicial system ignore us ritual survivors! I now can tell you exactly how abusers like that get away with it. The abuse for most people is so severe that the mind splits off to be able to survive it. This phenomenon is called MPD. Let's face facts here, who is going to believe someone with MPD? Who believes children usually? These are major reasons why they get away with it.

This is what I was facing, this is what I was thinking, and all of this were the reasons why I was angry and thought I could do nothing about it.

I went back to the bookstores. Again, I found very little that was actually helpful to me at my particular stage of grief. If there was something, I could not find it. There were plenty of books on people's experiences, which were comforting to the point of "misery loves company" or, in other words, just knowing I was not alone. That kind of information was not enough. I needed to move on. I needed to know how to leave my state of anger and walk into a state of peace.

Over and over again, I asked myself how I could stop being angry. Many other women I knew had been angry for decades, and they all said that they could not be anything but angry. My anger was valid, as was theirs. Some trauma survivors that I talked to said that they could not possibly find a way to not be angry, and that it would be impossible to even try! Some said it was their right to be angry and that God would understand and not hold them liable.

Because I am also a survivor, I know that I can comment on this type of thinking. God understands our anger, but after a time, He commands us to relinquish our anger and forgive even the vilest offender. God does not hold us accountable for what others do, but He does hold us responsible for how we respond to it. How to forgive and relinquish our anger is simple, we just obey and do it.

I can't is not an option here. After a period of grief and anger, we all *can* move on if we want to. It is an act of the will, just like Peter deciding to put on his shoes and follow the angel. He chose to do it.

Relinquishing our anger and forgiving does not mean that what they did is okay or that they don't deserve punishment, it just means that God (and sometimes our judicial system) gets to judge and punish the violators, not us. Let's face facts here, God can punish your offenders much better than you ever can ! Why not relinquish our anger? After all, when we are angry with our abductors and abusers, does it really hurt them? No, it does not hurt them if we stay angry, it just hurts us! Which of course was their intention! They love it when we suffer, or they would not have hurt us in the first place.

There are too many scriptures that tell us that our God is a god of justice and will punish the people that hurt you. Those that hurt us do not go unpunished. Relinquishing my anger does not mean that I have to trust them. Relinquishing my anger does not mean I have to spend time with them. Relinquishing my anger does not mean I have to talk to them. Relinquishing my anger is for me. It benefits me, not them. I have read the Bible cover to cover many, many times and I have never seen where I have to trust and have fellowship with someone who has proven themselves to be untrustworthy. What I do have to do is pray for them and let my anger go. As I pondered and thought on these truths, I was more upset by how difficult this obedience is than whether or not I should do it! Letting it go is not easy, it is difficult. I thought about my father-in-law, the man I described in the first chapter. At this point, he had not yet taken his life, but had alienated almost everyone he used to love, and I think that most of the people he was angry with were just like me, that is, they had no idea what they did to anger him. His anger was more important to him than his relationships. Trauma can do that to us all. I took a good hard look at myself and I realized that my anger was affecting my relationships also. I did not want to end up like my father-in-law, but I knew that I would indeed be very much like that if I did not find a viable solution. That solution was a choice to obey God.

I knew what I should do, but as with everything else in my life, I seem to foolishly try all other doors, try all the avenues, make all the mistakes, till I finally looked to the obvious solution. I wanted the easy way to feel better, instead of relinquishing my anger which is difficult. I knew what I had to do. I just did not want to do it. I hoped maybe that God would not need me to be obedient this time. I begged and begged God to "punish" those wicked people. I thought that if I could see them being punished, then letting go would be easier. Time passed and I kept on reading the Scriptures and hoping that I could find a solution other than having to do a simple yet hard act of obedience. I found none. I did read passages about God's judgment like Deuteronomy 32:35 which says:

> To me belongeth vengeance, and recompense; their foot shall slide in due time: for the day of their calamity is at hand, and the things that shall Come upon them make haste.

Okay, all those wicked people that hurt me will get what is coming to them. I did not feel better. So they get what they deserve. It will not change the fact that I am still a damaged person with big anger issues. If all of them burn in hell or get slowly tortured by being nibbled to death by a flock of geese, it really would not change my present circumstances in the least, would it? I got mad again. I knew all of the truths of obedience in forgiveness and anger issues, they are the truths that I have previously stated in this chapter. At this point, I still was not choosing to accept them. I was being stubborn. I would rather suffer than obey God because, at that time, I thought my suffering was less painful. This was not one of the smartest decisions that I have ever made.

Then I remembered that the objective of my abductors was to destroy me. I dusted myself off, got back into the Word, and was more determined than ever to stop being angry and obey God.

I knew then that God was not making me relinquish my anger because he is a mean God that does not care for my feelings, I knew then that God wants me to relinquish my anger because if I do not, the evil done to me continues on. I just keep reliving the pain if I do not choose to stop being angry.

It gave me great comfort to read about others in the Bible that had suffered great persecutions and hardships and unfair situations. The Bible is full of stories of people who had unfair and tough times and Jesus suffered more unfairly than any of us ever could.

In the New Testament, I could identify with the persecution of Paul and Peter because satanic abuse is definitely a form of persecution. I felt that I had a sisterhood going with some of the people that I read about in Acts. I contemplated the story of Stephen being stoned for his faith. Job certainly did not deserve the trials he endured, and we know this because the scripture tells us this. As I read and studied, I thought that no one quite says, "I am a member of the club of misery" quite like David does. According to the Old Testament scripture, David was a man after God's own heart. He made mistakes, but it seems to me that basically he was a good man who tried his best to do right by God

I think David had some really bad "breaks." He was the youngest of a bunch of boys who clearly were used to picking on him, and when God did help him to do something great (like killing Goliath), the jealousy of some others was very trying and sometimes emotionally painful. I found Psalm after Psalm, authored by David, pouring out his heart, expressing pain, misery, betrayal, and uncertainty. David tells us in great detail what it is like to be in emotional pain. I could really identify with David. As I was writing this, I had great difficulty in choosing just one Psalm to include in this subject, as there are so many that would fit the theme. I read so many that would be perfect at expressing how survivors feel, but I have chosen Psalm 34. I find great comfort in this Psalm because it tells me that "God gets it." He understands my pain and he is not happy with those who enjoy hurting people. I am including the reading of Psalm 34 in your action plan; make sure you read it, as I think it will give you great comfort. When we are born onto this earth, God gives us all the gift of "choices." We have a vast array of things to do good and evil, the choice is ours. I can choose, you can choose, the people that hurt us certainly have made some bad choices, but the choices were all their own. God is not pleased with bad choices, but we all have the power to do bad and stupid stuff. I am reminded of this truth every time I fly and have to go through airport security. Sometimes, an evil person's choices affect us all, and we all have to pay for it in long, tedious, demeaning hours of time that we can never get back

Psalm 34 tells me that God understands my plight, but it also gives me a clue to the answers that I so desperately need.

Psalm 34:22 says, "But the Lord is my defense; and my God is the rock of my refuge."

I read this and then "I got it" and true understanding started to emerge in my mind. In my head, things started to come together, pieces fitting, anger abating. The solution is simplistic in concept but takes practice and determination to pull it off, and here is the solution, anger is an attitude.

Before you are tempted to reject the solution, look at Psalm 34:22 again. It says that God is my defense, but I know you might be wondering how is he defending you.

In Ephesians 6:16, we are told to take up the shield of faith, wherewith we can withstand all the fiery darts of the wicked. I do not think that the main "darts" are the actual abuse, I think the main darts are what comes after, that is, the fear, anger, and loss. The physical pain ends but the devil uses fiery darts to keep the incidents fresh in our minds. This way, the devil knows that we get to keep experiencing the horror, thus crippling our lives.

Anger is a fiery dart. Anger is a way to cripple my life. Anger is a way to destroy me. Anger is a weapon of the enemy slung at me in the form of a suggestive attitude for the purpose of harming me and everyone that I love. Anger rarely affects the one who hurt us, in fact, the one we are angry with seldom notices that we are angry. If they do notice, they rarely care.

If the person or persons you are angry with are no longer part of your life, your anger is even more benign. They are most likely not even aware of your anger, so what good is it? Taking your anger out on people who did not cause you pain certainly is not smart, so why keep the anger around?

If anger is basically an attitude, I have hope because I can do something about my attitudes. No one can *make* me angry, I can choose to be angry. Anger is an attitude and nobody can control any of our attitudes. Our attitudes are choices that are all our own.

I think attitudes and choices are much easier when we take up that shield of faith. I needed to consciously exercise my faith by picking up my faith and using it. When I spent more time in the Word of God and focused on Him and chose to have the faith to know that he would put all this right, everything got easier. I began to have a peace with God that I never had before, and I was not angry. I am not going to lie to you and tell you that I have never again had an angry moment. I have been angry at things at times, but I always know that no one *made* me get angry, I chose to be angry. Knowing that anger is a choice is very empowering. I do not feel helpless when I make the choice to be angry, and I know that I can soon make the decision to stop being angry, and I always do. Even Jesus got angry a few times. He demonstrated to us that people do choose to get angry at times, and they can just as easily choose not to be angry. Anger takes up too much of my time and energy and really does not accomplish anything that I wish it would, so why keep it? Exercising faith helps of course, and faith is simply belief and trust. Peter trusted and believed when he was in prison. Peter did not sit in a corner and cry to the angel about how awful he had been treated. If Peter had displayed a burst of anger, could he have gotten out of prison? I think that the angry tirade may have kept him right the in the cell, chained to the guards. If Peter had decided to act out his anger by kicking the guards, hitting them, or yelling at them, would he have been able to get out? May I suggest to you that stuck in anger is a prison cell that you will be happy to leave. As long as we kick, hit, scream, and throw tantrums, we stay right there in the cell, even if the kicking, hitting, and yelling is only in our minds. When my children were toddlers, they all tried that kind of tantrum. I quickly learned that if I did not give in to their angry demands, they soon tired of the tactic and were more manageable. Even a two-year-old soon figures out that anger takes a lot of energy, especially if they do not get what they want. I do not think that there is anywhere in scripture that tells us that God gives into our angry demands and tirades. I have found the opposite to be true.

Whenever I have allowed my anger to spill over into my prayer life, it appears to me as if God "leaves the room" till I get control of myself. Too often after my bout of anger subsides, have I heard the Holy Spirit say, "Are you through now? Are you ready to listen? Or do you just prefer to keep up the tantrum? If you are through with the tantrum now, we can solve this problem."

Anger is defiantly a choice. I think we all can follow the example of Peter in prison and take our shield of faith and walk out of the prison. In the future, I decided to look at everything differently. I realized that most subjects and incidents are just not worthy of an argument. Most things in life that so many of us get angry about are just not worth the time it takes to justify the tantrum. If I choose to get angry with someone, I know it will take up time in my life that I can never get back. Moving on is usually smarter. Be careful to realize that stuffing and repressing anger means that I am still angry. If I stuff and repress my anger, it just means that I am pretending not to be angry. This, practiced over a lengthy time, is unhealthy emotionally and physically. Choosing not to be angry means that I am not angry outside or inside. It means that there is no reaction, even when there is no one to see. If you are not sure whether you have moved on from all your anger, this is a subject you need to explore with your therapist, pastor, best friend, or even your spouse. Your spouse always knows if you are repressing anger. Everyone feels better when angry feelings do not control them

Action Plan

1. Read all of Psalm 34.

2. Read Psalm 147:3–20.

3. Choose to relinquish your anger, ask God to help you in this matter.

4. Make a list of all the things you are angry about. At each point of anger, surrender this to the Lord and pray for the person you are angry with. The person(s) you are angry with need Jesus more than you can imagine. The Lord is so grieved by their behavior and it pleases Him to hear you pray for their souls. your objective in this exercise is to please the Lord, which will in turn make Him wish to bless you for your obedience. This is a milestone in your personal healing.

5. Remember that relinquishing anger is not for them, but blesses you. And as you do these exercises, you are singing in the night, making sweet melodies to God and your soul is healing some more.

6. Think about the fact that anger is always caused when there is something we want but cannot have.

I know that God always hears our prayers and praise, but I think we are especially dear to His heart when we sing and praise when life has not treated us in the best ways. Let your anger go, you will be glad you did.

21

Forgive

I sometimes think forgiving those who have so horribly used us is one of the hardest things for most of us to do in life. I know for sure that it is an important thing to do if you want to heal emotionally.

I believe that we think that if we forgive them, then we are saying that what they did was okay and they should not have consequences. I have searched the scriptures over and over and read to see if when we forgive others, they are off the hook. I find no place in the Bible that says if we forgive others that they automatically do not have to suffer consequences and are off the hook. The only one who has true power to forgive sins and erase the consequences is Jesus Christ.

When we repent of our sins and accept him as our Savior and Lord, he erases the consequences and forgives us fully. Jesus paid all the consequences of our sins when he was crucified. We know that we shall no longer be punished for our sins because he rose from the dead.

If the person/s who traumatized you have accepted Jesus's payment for their sin, repented, and made him Lord of their life, then they are forgiven indeed. This infuriates some survivors. Sometimes, a survivor would rather not have the people who traumatized them to be forgiven until they have been thoroughly punished. I understand your thinking, but it is unbiblical. Unfortunately, according to scripture, God might not bless the life of someone who thinks this way, which depresses many survivors because forgiving the evil people seems unfair and unreasonable to them. Before I go on, may I remind you that Jesus dying on the cross and paying the price for your sin and mine seems unfair and unreasonable in the extreme. For me, learning to have the mind of God in the forgiveness matter was difficult to sort out, but when I finally figured it out and learned the mind of God in the matter, it became relatively easy to do.

Let us first make a list of what forgiveness is not when the person/s who traumatized you does not love God or want anything to do with him. When the persons do not love God, forgiveness does not mean that what they did was okay.

1. That they should not suffer consequences or be punished.

2. That I should be "friends" with them.

3. That I trust them.

That I am expected to trust them or have any type of relationship with them. When you forgive others their sins against you, it means that you let it go and let God handle the punishment or maybe the judicial system if you can. I am not saying that if someone in the mall parking lot tries to force you into their car that you should not defend yourself, I am saying that forgiving others when they have sinned against you is good for you. Your forgiveness probably will not benefit them, it benefits you. I think that the scripture teaches us that forgiveness is an act of obedience and is a choice we make.

> For if ye forgive men their trespasses; your heavenly Father will also forgive you. But if ye forgive not men their trespasses, neither will your Father forgive your trespasses. (Matthew 6 :14, 15)

Unfortunately, I see nothing in the scripture above that exempts a trauma survivor. There are many people out there that are holding back forgiveness for much lesser charges, and I see no place in the Bible that says this is okay either. The station of forgiveness is a place where a vast number of people stay and never reach the gates of healing. This obedience of forgiveness is the last stop to the gates. Anyone can see the iron gates now, but they will not open until this act of the will is completed. No one can shove the gates open, this is something God has to do, and he will do it for anyone who completes this last thing. I could always find a way to argue my way out of forgiving the devil worshipers until I remembered that my sin debt to God was far greater than anything they had done to me. Forgiveness means that I have given the burden of pain back to the almighty God and relinquished my hate.

Forgiveness is a right heart with God, not a reconciliation with those who abused me. Forgiveness is not pretending that the trauma never happened. Forgiveness is giving the whole mess to God and making it his problem, not mine. I think most people can recite the Lord's Prayer. It begins with "Our Father who art in heaven," and goes on from there. I doubt that too many people have actually stopped to meditate on the verses much. The verses are comforting, but I think that there is admonishing in the verses as well. Matthew 6:12 of the Lord's Prayer says, "And forgive us our debts (can be translated as trespasses, or sins) as we forgive our debtors." It was a new revelation to me one day as I saw something in this passage that I had always ignored. I realized for the first time that we are asking God to forgive us in the exact same way that we forgive others, hence, as we forgive our debtors. I thought that if I was asking God to forgive me in the same way that I was forgiving, that I was in big trouble, as forgiveness was not something that at that time I was giving freely. I was believing the lie, thinking that if I do not forgive those who wronged me, I was keeping myself safe, so that it would not happen again. I came to the conclusion that this was indeed erroneous thinking. Holding on to my anger and unforgiveness was no kind of reasonable defense against wickedness.

In the Lord's Prayer, we are essentially asking God to forgive us in the same way that we forgive others. So if we have not forgiven others, God will not forgive us either and then we can cut ourselves out of blessings.

The Bible says to pray for them who persecute you and despitefully use you (Matthew 5:44, Luke 6:27–28, Romans 12:14–21). I found this concept easy to digest but difficult to do. Doing this took prayer and determination.

I prayed for all those who have hurt me. I prayed for God to send them the right people and circumstances to lead them to Him. I prayed that they would trust God and repent of their sin and accept Jesus as their savior and payment for their sins. After I sincerely prayed for all I could think of, I felt much lighter in my spirit and I know that I had forgiven indeed. The choice was now theirs whether to accept the grace of God or continue in their sin. Now, every time someone wrongs me, I see it as an opportunity to pray for their salvation and enlightenment.

I think that if we look at all this from God's point of view, things not only look different but really come into perspective. From God's point of view, it hurts him terribly when someone wrongs us. If you study the scriptures well, I think you will agree with me in that, it hurts God far more than it hurts us, no matter what was done to us. I think that when we are angry, hateful, and unforgiving, year after year, it just intensifies his pain. I do not want to hurt my Lord's feelings, I have come to love him too much. If anyone thinks that God does not have feelings, it is apparent that they have not read the Bible very carefully yet because the Bible is full of God's feelings. The scriptures plainly tell us that he feels sorrow, love, joy, remorse, anger, hate, pity, compassion, jealousy, and many more emotions that we humans can identify with. When I think of God in that light, I am more careful with my actions and thoughts, as I do not want to hurt his feelings. I know that he understands our feelings of anger, hate, and unforgiveness because he knows how much we were hurt, but to prolong those feelings and hurts ultimately can partially separate us from him. I want to be as close to God as I can because I have learned that when I separate myself from him, I do stupid stuff. Staying close to him helps me to be wise in my finances, relationships, and all decisions. Staying close to God keeps me out of a lot of trouble, but the nicest advantage of staying close to him is the comfort he brings me when I do not get too far away.

Forgiving others benefits me. Forgiving others strengthens me. Forgiving others makes my burdens lighter. Forgiving others opens the iron gates of freedom. Forgiving others is an act of obedience.

Action Plan

1. Read Matthew 5:44, Luke 6: 27, Romans 12:14–21, Psalms 25:18.

2. Forgive your enemies and all who wronged you and walk through the gates.

3. Read Luke 11:4.

4. Read Matthew 18:23–35.

Remember that unforgiveness keeps us in bondage. The gates of healing cannot and will not open until we obey God and forgive those that have wronged us.

22

Circumstances

It seems that there is always someone who thinks that because of their circumstances, God will change the rules just for them. They think that they are the only ones who have suffered this much, so God will automatically not expect them to obey the scriptures. I have talked to so many people that even think that criminals should be protected and excused from their behavior because those criminals had such a bad childhood. Sometimes people believe the lie that says, "Sometimes we just cannot help it, because of our past or even present circumstances, we are exempt from doing the right thing." May I say here, that God has promised us that He will always give us everything we need to be righteous, and those that say they cannot because of their circumstances and past life are calling God a liar. I am sorry to have to sound so harsh, but I must agree with the Bible on this subject. After searching the scriptures and consulting many Bible scholars, I have come to the conclusion that there is no human being that has a God-given excuse to do as they please. In this writing, I have not included most of the rough and unfair and difficult circumstances that I had to live through. Because I am a member of the "I survived a million unfair and traumatic experiences" club, I think I am qualified to make these statements, but I promise you that it was not an easy truth to embrace.

At times, we all wish to use our trauma as an excuse to do as we please, chiefly because it is usually easier to do the wrong thing. None of us likes the hard way and the difficult path, which is what we sometimes have to walk on if we wish to do the righteous and good things.

The Bible is abundant with people thinking that, in this one case, God will understand my circumstances and excuse me from obeying the truth. I have learned the hard way, that is kind of thinking comes right out of the pit of hell.

> I can do all things through Christ which strengtheneth me. (Philippians 4:13)

Remember back to chapter 5 about Peter in prison. God will do for you what you cannot, you will be required to do what you can. You might stay at certain stations for a while as you pass through the corridors, but the Bible says that because of Jesus, all of us have the strength and resources to perform each task, even the difficult ones.

When a task seems difficult, it is so much easier to decide that we cannot do it and think that God will understand. We refuse to believe the truth, in that, God will give us more strength and grace to do his will. God will always give us all we need to perform the task at hand, and he is always happy to do it, we just need to ask.

The good news is that God will patiently wait for us to do what we can, the choice is ours. God will never command us to do something that is impossible for us to do. What he commands might be difficult at times, but never impossible. I have sat through enough group therapy sessions and have heard all the excuses people use to not heal. They feel support within the group and that is enough for them. They do not want complete healing because that might require them to do something difficult, and because of what they suffered, they think it would be unfair of God to ask them to do this difficult thing, and therefore, they are sure that in this circumstance, he will excuse them. I used to feel that way myself.

I have sat in some therapy groups where the majority of the women in the group were condoning the sinful behavior of a particular lady because after all "she has been through so much, this behavior is understandable and God will ignore it." This is a good place to remind those with that mind-set that it angers God for anyone to teach that sin is okay.

I have lived long enough to see many churches split over this concept. There are always plenty of folks out there that think that God did not mean what he said. They pick and choose the parts of scripture they like and discard the parts they do not like.

In the church splits that I have known about, the two sides always face off with the same argument. One side says, "God said it, we must obey it"; the other side argues that God will recognize the unique circumstances (is there really such a thing as unique circumstances?) and let this one slide. I must warn you here that if you choose to stay engaged in sinful behavior using your past as an excuse, that you will completely stop your healing and stay stagnant. Believe me, if there had been away to get around some of the healing concepts I would have found them. Shortcuts through the prison corridors just do not exist, we either choose to do them or we choose not to, it is really quite simple. My last psychologist, the one I mentioned at the beginning of this book, told me that not too many people he had counseled were willing to do the difficult things as I was. He said that I am unusual and wished that all of his clients were willing to obey the scriptures so that they would know the amazing feelings of healing. I do not consider myself special in those regards, and I certainly do not consider myself to be without sin. I have made plenty of mistakes in my lifetime and do not consider myself to be some unusual spiritual giant. I think I am probably just like most Christians, trying to live my best life, working out my salvation daily, and sometimes, it is not easy to do the right thing. I included this chapter to try and persuade some who may think that the Lord will excuse them from the hard things like anger and forgiveness, then choose not to do them, and then be upset because the gates have not opened.

My wish and prayer for all who hear my story will find hope and know that God will always do for you what you cannot do. He is good and loving and does not wish anyone to feel hurt and pain.

Action Plan

1. Read 1 Corinthians 9:22–27.

2. Memorize 2 Corinthians 12:10.

3. Read 1 Peter 3:18–22.

4. Read 1 Peter 4:1–13.

23

Know Your Enemy

For we wrestle not with flesh and blood, but against
principalities, against powers, against the rulers of darkness
in high places. (Ephesians 6:12)

Emotional and physical trauma of any person is like an octopus
with far-reaching tentacles. Our enemy, the devil, knows this truth
and uses it to his best advantage. I do not know what percentage
of people do not believe in the devil, but I personally know that
he is real. For those of you who do not believe what the Bible
says about a literal devil and enemy of mankind, please at least
hear me out instead of skipping this all important chapter. As a
survivor of satanic ritual abuse, I think that I have some authority
to talk on this subject. Satan does exist, demons do exist, evil
is present, and we know this because the Bible warns us about
these things. The word of God says that the devil is a roaring
lion, seeking whom he may devour (1 Peter 5:8). Any military
strategist knows that you need to know who your enemy is. Every
army has people who study the enemy and learn as much as they
can about their enemy's tactics. The more you know about your
enemy and its tactics, the less effective he is and your chances for
victory increase. In this case, your victory is healing.

Again, looking at Ephesians 6: 12, the Bible says that we
wrestle (or fight) not with flesh and blood, but against something
far more powerful and scary. Those people who say that a loving
God would not have a devil roaming the earth are misinformed.

Most of us survivors do not really have too difficult a time knowing that a devil is present. For most people who have been traumatized and ill used, the question is not about existence of the devil and evil, it is more a question of, "How do I deal with the past, present, and future evil?" I believe that the Bible is full of answers, but my favorite verses are in Ephesians 6. Ephesians 6:11 tells us to put on the whole armor of God that you may be able to stand against the wiles of the devil. I think that it is interesting to note that two verses later says:

> Wherefore take unto you the whole armor of God, that you may be able to stand in the evil day, and having done all, to stand.

I think that if this same concept is repeated again so soon, that it must be important to God and to us especially. Apparently, God did not want us to miss this.

I believe that the reason this thought is repeated again so quickly is because the enemy is empowered when we do not do right. In the particular subject of healing, if we are not following the strategy of the Bible, that is, responding rightly to circumstances and attitudes, we give place to the devil and give him more power to hurt and annoy us. If you do not believe this, think of the people and circumstances that orchestrated your trauma. They were choosing to do the evil that your enemy wanted, causing you much pain. The point here is that we need to recognize the enemy and take charge over ourselves like any other warrior. As I previously stated, we need to know who our enemy is and then we need to formulate a plan to defeat him. No country going to war just invades and shoots, they make a plan and a strategy. They study who the enemy is, what he does, what he likes, what his objectives are, and what his weaknesses are. The person/s who caused you such pain probably had a plan. I know that the people who caused my trauma definitely had a plan. They fact that they had stalked me is quite clear.

In some cases, this is not true; there are random rapes, murders, and muggings, of course. My daughter Joy, who majored in criminology when she was in law school, says that the random acts of violence are the most difficult to get a conviction on because the police simply have so few leads to follow. The people who violated you might not have had a plan, but the devil did, he always does. He knows who you are, studies where you will be, what your weaknesses are, where your strengths lie, and how he can best hurt you or use you to hurt others. He is the lion who devours and destroys. The devil was empowered because the people who hurt you were happy to do evil and chose not to do right. Satan will go for the weak hearted and the weak in faith. Wherever there is weakness, the devil will focus in on that. When my granddaughter, Ava, was just four years old, her family, with Mark and I, took her to the zoo. We were all enjoying our trip to the zoo and decided to look at the mountain lion exhibit. We really did not linger too long at first, mostly because mountain lions are not a big deal to Mark and I as we can sometimes see them in the wild where we live. I am wary and nervous around mountain lions, even if they are behind glass.

As we were walking past the lion enclosure, I watched the big cat watching us! One by one, we filed past, my son Joel, his wife, Mark, and granddaughter Alyx, walked past with the cat looking at us, but clearly showing very little interest. Ava was in front of me, and as she walked past the enclosure, the cat suddenly changed its demeanor. I watched the lion pick up her ears, tense her muscles, and carefully watch and follow every movement of our Ava.

We all noticed the change in the cat then and encouraged Ava to walk back and forth past the lion to see what would happen. The rest of us in the party were too big and looked too strong to captivate the lion's attention, but evidently, Ava looked weak, small, and just the right bite size. This incident was really making me feel uncomfortable. I was reminded of 1 Peter 5:8 about the devil like a lion seeking whom he may devour. Lions, like the devil, are not as likely to pick on someone who is not an easy target. Lions and devils go for the weak spots as well as the easy meals. As I stated in chapter 8, about boundaries, a mountain lion will seldom, if ever, attack a full-grown horse, but a lame or weak-looking one can be a target. The devil, as a roaring lion, does not play fair; he will look for where you are weak, then attack you there. Sin always creates weakness in us. James 1:14 says that every man is tempted when he is drawn away of his own lust and enticed. Our hidden lusts and wishes and anything that is not of God are our weaknesses. All of us have weaknesses that we must eradicate if we are to live victorious lives. Weakness can take many forms. Lies, deceit, envy, murder, thievery, fornication, adultery, dishonoring parents, coveting, and on and on the list goes. We are all guilty of something sometime and the devil comes back to where he had victory before. I am not weak in all these things and neither are you, but the devil knows where we *are* weak. Anger and unforgiveness in us are weaknesses that the devil can use to do us unimaginable heartbreak. Most survivors have the most problems in these two areas. If you are still struggling with these, revisit the last three chapters and live at that station till you have complete victory. Gaining victory over your anger and unforgiveness will be part of your plan of action to keep the devil's tactics at minimum or squash them altogether.

Satan has limited power, but he has unlimited influence, if we let him influence us. We all have the choice to listen to suggestions of evil or to ignore them. There was a TV show in the 1970s where the host was always saying, "The devil made me do it." This TV personality was very entertaining but highly misinformed. The devil cannot make us do anything. We as human beings can choose to do right or wrong.

The point to understand here is that the devil's objective when we were traumatized was to encourage the person/s who injured you to do as much damage as they could, so that your whole life, and maybe the lives of others also, could be crippled, miserable, and destroyed. Evil had its plans and now you need a success plan. The great news here is that God has already made a plan for you to achieve victory over this enemy. You do what you can, and He will do the rest. Your life is not over and you can feel good. There is a military-style plan laid out in Ephesians 6. Study and memorize this plan of defense as a way to enjoy your time outside the iron gates. No one wants to be trapped inside again. This strategy will give you more strength and tools to live a victorious life. The Ephesians 6 strategy empowers you if you but implement it.

I went through much of my life feeling powerless. Feeling powerless is victim thinking, a victim mentality. I could and did reclaim my power when I started living Ephesians 6, and I believe that that kind of power is available to us all. Just doing something opposite of the pain we know can give us an amazing sense of power.

First of all (Ephesians 6:14), having your loins gird about with truth and having the breastplate of righteousness. Truth is the number 1 strategy against evil. All of evil begins with a lie. Stop here for just a moment and think about the lies that led to your own trauma. Do not dwell on the lies, just recognize that they existed. Your particular trauma may not have seemed to start with and without lies, maybe you just did not have all the information you needed to stay safe and protected. However, you can be sure that behind the trauma was the devil, whispering to your assailant, who was only too willing to comply. Information is power. Truth is power. Ephesians 6:14 says, "Having your loins gird about with truth." Where you get this truth is simple, you get truth from God and he gave us his word, which is the Bible. I have found that God will not lie to me ever. God is incapable of lies.

The Bible is full of good things for all, comfort, information, truth, and empowerment. I doubt that any of us use this all-powerful tool to its full potential. If most of us or even a small percentage of us were truly using the wisdom of God's word in every capacity, there would be a lot less misery in this world. When I finally figured out that I was not using everything God gave me to fullest potential, I was extremely annoyed with myself. I thought of all the misery I had suffered in my life, simply because I did not apply the truth of the Word of God. It was there all the time, I just was not using it. I had untold wealth, but was sometimes living in spiritual poverty just because I was not fully reading and applying what God had provided. Ignorance is not always bliss, sometimes it can be lethal.

Begin each day and before you go to bed with praise and a reading of the word. I have found that the simple exercise of starting the day on a high note makes the whole day better. Scripture reading before sleep can possibly minimize or eliminate night terrors. This strategy has always helped me. The devil would like you to focus on your past so that he can best use you and cripple you. Like the Bible instructs us, speak to yourself in Psalms and hymns and spiritual songs. Meditate on the Word, and of all things, of course, practice gratitude and praise to God, the devil hates these and they will cripple him. I think that the things that the devil hates more than Jesus Christ are praise and gratitude.

Be wary and watchful and pay attention with prayer at all times (Ephesians 6:18). As a survivor of satanic ritual abuse, I know for a fact that in most churches today, members of the satanic covens are planted in churches to cause trouble. They attend church, learning the talk, pretending to follow right living, but all the while looking for how they can cause harm to the children of God. If you feel uncomfortable with certain people in a church setting, pray for them, watch them, and be careful. Keep focused on the Word of God, not these people, in this way, you are having your feet shod with the preparation of the gospel of peace (Ephesians 6: 15), and sometimes, these people actually accept Jesus and turn away from their devil worship. I have actually talked to some of these people, and what an amazing testimony it is to the churches and people who led them to the truth!

As you get closer and closer to God, you will more easily recognize the people that the devil has a good influence on. As you recognize them and in humility pray for them, the devil's influence through them can be drastically minimized. Sophisticated espionage always involves spies and troublemakers, and those of us who have survived are always considered targets for more pain. The devil knows that he victimized you once and it worked, so he wants to stay with what worked. Be vigilant and ask God to put the angels of protection around you and around your family, exercising your faith in God to protect you (Ephesians 6:16).

All survivors need to exercise faith. Think of faith as billions of dollars in the bank just waiting for you to withdraw and use it. We all actually do have untold riches at our disposal in the Bible. If you were to have a bank account with billions of dollars in your name and you want to use some, you would need to write a certificate of withdrawal and hand it to the teller, which at that time the teller at the bank would hand you your money. Think of faith as your certificate of withdrawal. Faith is my response to what God has already done and provided. When I exercise my faith, I am presenting my heavenly account with my certificate of withdrawal. Faith is the opposite of fear. A great many survivors are plagued with fear. Not just fear of what may happen, but fearing to give up anger and unforgiveness because we think that holding on to these keeps us safer. My faith tells me that everything that has happened in my life, that was beyond my control, good or evil, is part of who I have become. I can let the negative things destroy me, or I can exercise faith in the power of God to let those things renew me. I can let fear destroy me by constantly expecting more traumas, or I can exercise faith by letting my trauma be a tool for learning, growing, and keeping me safe.

Anger and unforgiveness reveals itself in the form of fear. Faith shatters fear.

I need to have faith that Romans 8:28 is true when it says that *all* things work together for good to them that love God. The devil means to hurt and destroy, but every negative thing can be turned into a positive if we have the faith to just look for the good. An example of this would be the story of Joseph in the book of Genesis chapters 37 to 45.

The story of Joseph could have turned out much different if Joseph had not exercised faith.

There was a time, I must admit, when I look back, that I could not see how any of the suffering that I endured could ever be good. When I was first working through all of my issues and feeling so raw with negative emotions, the only faith I had was to believe that I would be whole someday. I just kept trusting in faith that God would make it right. But now, the past has no hold on me anymore. Faith is the shield in our arsenal of tools to defend ourselves against the devil.

Ephesians 6:17 gives us another piece of armor. It says to take the helmet of salvation. God is telling us to make sure that we really do have a relationship with him and not just a religion. God is saying to make sure that we are connected to the Son of God and truly plugged into the power. If you are still not sure about what this means, refer back to chapter 4.

The rest of verse 17 tells us to take up the sword of the spirit, which is the Word of God. All the other warrior's weapons are defensive, I think that the sword of the spirit is offensive. A sword can cut, hurt, and kill. The sword is meant to destroy evil in our lives as well as protect us. God's word (the Bible) can and does do major damage to evil concepts if it is in the hands of a skilled warrior. If you still think that you do not need to start the day with Bible reading, I hope the fact that the Word of God is the sword to help you do battle will convince you. Learn the Word and learn to be a skilled soldier, using the words of the Bible to destroy the hurt, depression, despair, anxiety, fear, and anger within you. You can talk to your therapist for decades, recounting your times of torture and fear, but they still might not go away. When you actively attack all those same feelings with the sword of the spirit, which is the Word of God, you will begin to feel differently. How much difference you feel and how much healing you attain will be up to you and how much you are willing to use your "sword." Remember Peter in prison, God has supplied the sword of the spirit (Bible), you need to take it and use it. The Word of God is a mighty sword to anyone smart enough to pick it up and use it.

Jesus knew this truth well and he illustrated this truth in Matthew 4:1–11. In this passage, when Jesus was tempted in the wilderness, the Bible tells us that with each temptation that the devil threw at him, Jesus used the scriptures to defeat the devil. Jesus showed us how to defeat the enemy with the shield of faith and the sword of the spirit.

In Ephesians 6:14, God tells us to *stand*. Warriors do not lie down and sit idly, they take a position suited for battle. I think this means for us to be ready and watchful. A standing position is a ready position.

Action Plan and Assignment

1. Read Matthew 4:1–11.

2. Read Daniel 10:12–13.

3. Read 2 Corinthians 4:4–18.

4. Read Ephesians 6:10–18.

5. Thank your loving heavenly Father because you know that through all of this difficult deployment, you have opportunity to grow stronger and closer to Him.

6. Read 1Corinthians 2:7–8.

7. Read James 4:7.

8. Read 1 Peter 5:8.

24

The Medicine of Self-Esteem

I have lived long enough to know that those of us who have had trauma at a young age and especially trauma that involves rape or molestation have difficulty with self-esteem. I think that abuse can destroy your vision of what you are worth and who you are. It certainly did for me, but it matters little if you have had trauma, or not suffered trauma, it seems that the majority of people in this country suffer from some degree of poor self-image.

I personally had to come to the realization that, no matter what happened to me, no matter how I have been treated, no matter what talents, beauty, or brains that I may or may not possess, I have infinite worth and so does everyone else.

Why do we all think that everyone else has worth above measure, but when most of us look in the mirror, we make an exception. I am going to make a confession right now, I like movies and I like TV. I like to be entertained by these devices. I think that most of us do like it all, but most of us really do not want to admit that if TV were gone forever, those of us that grew up with it would miss it. If this were not true, the TV networks, actors, and sponsors would not be making so much money. They make money because most of us like their product. If the majority of us who say that we really do not watch too much, all of the sudden did what we said (that is did not watch too much), then Hollywood would be bankrupt and actors, producers, and promoters would not be living in mansions.

I am not saying that there is anything wrong with them all living in mansions, I am only trying to prove that yes, most of us do like the media, we support it, and the fact that they are living in elaborate conditions proves it. If most of us stopped watching, most of them might look for other jobs.

I am convinced that most of us indeed do watch or listen to the media more hours than we daily read our Bibles. I am working on making sure that my daily Bible reading is greater than media watching. I think that we all must get our priorities right.

As I was in the midst of my healing adventure, I made a startling observation. I figured out that part of the image I had of myself can be in direct correlation to the "stuff" I was filling my head with. The big problem was not the fact that I was watching TV, reading magazines, or listening to the radio, the big problem was that I was subconsciously believing all the junk that they were telling me. Couple that with a trauma at five years old and you have a prescription for low self-esteem. I think that most of us learn subconsciously from an early age that unless our hair is just right, our toothpaste the best, our perfume expensive, our clothes stylish, our weight below average, our skin flawless, our IQ above 150, our car new, our house immaculate, our laundry whitest, our electronics the latest, our jewelry the finest, our lawns the greenest, our holidays idyllic, our vacations amazing, our underwear the sexiest, our shave the closest, our pets the healthiest, our dishes without water spots, and our children wearing the best shoes, we are somehow just not worthy. And by the way, all of this has to be accomplished before we are forty years of age because after forty, according to media messages, we are just not worth as much, to society, ourselves or even God. But they tell us that we can make ourselves more acceptable if we all strive to look as if we are younger, and that is achieved by using their products. As you read this, I know you are thinking that all this is absurd, but subconsciously, chances are, you really believe it. We, because of advertising and the media, deep down inside of ourselves really do believe all this junk. I can make this statement with confidence because I know that if we did not believe all this nonsense, we all would have better self-esteems. When it comes to advertising, what is missing in the long list of what we need to be to be worthy is character, integrity, and a relationship with Jesus. Who nowadays thinks that that stuff is really important? Advertisers and entertainment media certainly do not think these things are very important, because if we already have good character and a relationship with Jesus, you might not need their stuff. After all, if we are happy in our relationship with Christ, wrinkle-free skin, whiter laundry, and children's adoration because we bought the right shoes will not be nearly as important.

In summary, if our self-esteem is healthy, the advertisers will not sell as much of their products. Yes, we will always need shampoo, toothpaste, laundry soap, and clothing, but they sell more of it if we feel that we are somehow lacking without their product. And of course, because we feel so bad about ourselves, we believe it! Deep down inside, as a people, we feel so bad about ourselves that we buy into the notion that if we just had that hair, those clothes, that car, or the idyllic holiday, we would not only feel better about ourselves, we might even accept and like ourselves. I am not saying that we should all stop reading magazines, watching TV, or listening to radio. I know that unless God specifically tells me not to or if the electric grid collapses, I will keep enjoying my favorite magazines and TV programs. I see nothing in scripture that says it is wrong, although I have seen advertisements for some programs and magazines that I think God is probably very displeased with. I avoid those things because the scripture tells us to keep away from the very appearance of evil. I try to be careful about what I "let into my head." However, morals here are not the point that I am trying to convey right now. The point is, that with whatever disadvantages we grew up with, such as not having the perfect parents (who in the world has a set of those?), media does not help us feel better about ourselves. The answer is not to mute out all the commercials, the smart attitude is to look at what they are selling, after all, you might need a new car, but to realistically know that what you wear, how you smell, what you drive, or where you live does not determine your worth. If those are the things that some others are judging you on, avoid those people. Nice stuff and flawless skin can make us feel good about ourselves, but it is only a temporary fleeting feeling. I like nice stuff, but it does not satisfy the innermost parts of me, like a relationship with Jesus does. It took me a long time to get to this point of acceptance of myself and the realization that I am worthy. Just because someone calls you stupid does not make it true, it makes them a liar.

Just because someone treats you with contempt does not make you unworthy, it makes them inconsiderate. Just because others pick on you and belittle you does not make you less, it makes them accountable to God someday for what they said. Just because others verbally put you down because they believe lies about you does not make you the lie, it makes them irresponsible with their tongue. Just because others have abused you physically does not mean you deserved it, it means that they are evil. When others abuse you verbally, abuse you mentally, or abuse you physically, it does not mean you are worthy of that treatment, it means that they are tools of the devil and enjoy hurting others.

Sadly, it ultimately means that their self-esteem is lower than yours because if they had healthy self-esteem, they would not be so cruel and mean. People who know who they are in Christ do not need to put other people down and hurt others to make themselves feel better. All of us at one time or another can be insensitive, but people who love Jesus do not do it intentionally. Evil people intentionally hurt you and then get pleasure when you feel bad. Evil people get pleasure from causing pain and sorrow. Why in the world do we allow evil people to determine our worth and value? I have never known an evil person that could go a whole day without telling a lie to hurt someone. Are we seriously going to let that kind of person decide what our worth is? The answer to the self-esteem problem that is intertwined with your trauma is:

1. Go back into your history and see the perpetrators for who they really are. In other words, are they really such amazing, wonderful, impeccable character people that they can accurately assess your worth?

2. Study what the Bible says about your worth and believe it.

3. Look at what Jesus has done for you and accept the fact that He would not have given so much for you if you were not priceless.

4. Choose to accept and like who you are.

If we keep thinking that we will accept and love ourselves when we achieve certain things or look a certain way, we will just keep moving the goal posts. After years and years of feeling inferior, I finally came to the conclusion that self-esteem was a choice. I decided that if I made provisos on when I would accept myself, I probably would never accept myself. I figured out that if we have decided that we must look a certain way, live in a certain area, be a certain age, land the dream job, win the guy or girl, achieve a great success in business, or win the prize before we accept ourselves, we will never achieve our goal because we will just make another goal. Self-esteem must not be external. It must not be based on what others think of us. If good self-esteem is to be based on what others think and say to us, then they better be as sinless as Jesus, because He is really the only one that can decide our worthiness. Giving the deciding of our worthiness to others is really silly. Are they perfect? Do they have perfect bodies? Have they achieved perfect success in business? Do they all have genius IQs? Are they sinless? Are they all knowing? What really gives others the right to judge us anyway? Why do we give away our power to accept ourselves to others? When did God die and put them in charge? I can take constructive criticism from my parents, husband, or certain business associates, if it makes me better. Most of the time, the criticism that others bestow on us is not intended to do us good, but to put us down and thereby making the critic feel better about himself. Usually, criticism and nasty remarks are void of truth and simply not constructive, rather they are destructive and are intended to destroy some part of me that someone else may be jealous of. I have carefully observed that if someone is doing unkind gossip, if you pay close attention, you will figure out that the gossiper is extremely jealous of the person that they are trying to destroy with their tongue.

The Bible is very clear on the subject of backbiters and jealousy, God says that it is sin and it is (James 3:14–16).

The first thing we can do to achieve a healthy self-esteem is to keep away from those that will tear us down with unkind remarks and deeds. (Refer back to the chapter on boundaries if you need to.) I made a firm decision to like myself enough to keep away from those people that enjoy running me down. Why should I care what others say about me? They are not God, and they do not have the truth. God knows who I am and He knows that I will own the mistakes and messes that I have made myself, but I will not let the devil destroy me because of what a few people who are not obeying God say about me that is untrue. I think this falls under the category of the death and life being in the power of the tongue (Proverbs 18: 21). But the good news is that I do not have to let the opinions and tongues of others destroy me or my self-esteem. I can make a different choice.

In your action plan, you will be asked to get a pen and paper and write down all of the untold truths declared over you. Then, one by one, deal with each for what it is, unkind and untrue. Many people that I have talked to were pronounced stupid, worthless, incorrigible, unnecessary, and a mistake by some acquaintances, family, and even teachers.

My mother used to tell me the rhyme, "Sticks and stones will break my bones but names will never hurt me." Well, I have come to believe that the negative nasty stuff that some people have declared about us does hurt more than sticks and stones. Many women in abusive relationships would rather be physically hit than beaten up with someone's hateful words. Initially, words do hurt, but when we look at them through the truth of Jesus Christ and decide that what was said is not truth, but indeed, the sin problem of the person delivering the insults, then it does not damage our self-esteem. Unfortunately, most of the time, we take the careless nastiness of others to heart without ever processing that garbage into truth. We are angry at them for saying it and obsess about it for a long time because we are afraid that deep inside, we might think that what was said is true, and we are taking our self-esteem from those around us, instead of the truth of Jesus. Some of us take the nastiness of others as truth because of our past trauma.

If we properly process the insensitive tongues of others through our action plans and the Biblical teachings, the insults should die there. But as I said, most of the time we just do not take the time to process it, and it festers and grows into problems with our self-esteem, buried deep into out subconscious minds, crippling our lives. Once you have processed the feelings and declared that the words spoken over you were garbage, then pray for those who said the hurtful things and you will feel some healing. The next thing to think about is the other way we rely on external affirmation to determine our self-worth. In other words, we can think we are less than acceptable by the negative things people say and do, such as in the previous paragraphs, and we can think we are less than acceptable by the things people do not say and do to and for us. Sometimes, people's self esteems are damaged by what they do *not* get from others. It can be as small as a compliment not paid that offends us and wrecks our self-esteem or as large as wanting the love of someone that will not return it to us.

As a people, we depend far too much on the good opinions and gestures of others to determine our self-worth. I certainly do not want to offend others, but if they are looking to me to give affirmation of their self-worth, I might fall short and disappoint them. The reason for this is because I am not Jesus Christ, and He is the only one that can truly validate us. That is not to say that I do not try to make others feel good about themselves. I can compliment others, and I can treat them with respect, and that is an affirmation of their self-worth. But a relationship with Jesus is the only real way that we can have complete and whole self-esteem.

I think that most of us have never sat down and actually thought about how often we rely on the good deeds and words of others to give us the affirmation that we all crave.

Ladies, when our husbands and boyfriends forget our birthday, why are we really upset? I can tell you why, because the gestures of others, such as birthdays and anniversaries remembered, gives us the affirmation we desire. He remembered my birthday and bought me a special present; therefore, I must be a desirable, good person! Well, for today that is, because in a few weeks, when our weak self-esteems need more help, it is possible that our mates will fail us, and we will fail them, if they are wholly looking to us for their self-esteem.

I wonder if fragile self-esteems are not the real cause of most affairs and divorces. I sometimes think that people honestly believe that the "love" of some certain person will finally complete them. May I suggest that only God can complete any of us. So many of us think that if we do not get enough praise at work or attention showered on us by our peers that we are somehow not worthy.

Most of us spend an infinite number of hours concocting new schemes and ways that we can be more acceptable to others, therefore, making us feel worthy when we get their praise and adoration. We think that we are not acceptable to our peers (and we need their acceptance to feel good), if we do not drive a certain car, live in a certain neighborhood, and any other number of insignificant things that we go into debt for, just because we want to be accepted. We think that unless we are accepted by the masses, we are not very good people. People are going into massive debt, thinking that their children, as well as themselves, need this thing or that thing, so that we can receive praise from others and, therefore, boosting our self-esteem. May I suggest that Proverbs 18:10 may be a beginning to help us recover our self-esteem. It says that, "The name of the Lord is a strong tower; the righteous runneth into it, and is safe." To get rid of a negative, we must replace it with a positive. I now know that the only way to have good self-esteem (and God wants us to have good self-esteem) is to look to Him. We will never reach enough goals or have enough admiration from others to fully get us the self-esteem we need. If all we needed was lots of money, stuff, looks, and admiration from an adoring public, then why do so many celebrities battle with addictions and go from marriage to marriage? If money, stuff, looks, intelligence, and admiration were really all we need, then you would *never* hear about celebrities with any problems because they certainly do have all that. But we are constantly hearing about celebrities in court and having big problems, the same ones the average person battles with. Affirmation from others and perfect stuff is not the answer.

Even though I know all of these truths in my head, it has been difficult to believe and live them until I learned fully how to praise God. For far too many years, I looked on the external things of what others said or did to and for me to determine my self-worth. I tried all the self-reformation things that are materialistic. I finally came to the conclusion that self-acceptance is a choice and I had to choose to accept myself in the light of the sacrifices that Jesus has done for me.

Anyone that thinks that they cannot accept themselves is letting the devil win. We can very well choose to have good self-esteem and we can do it because it pleases God. If we think of self-acceptance in the light of pleasing our Lord and how much it pleases Him, then we can do it. Good self-esteem is a command of God. In Matthew 22:37–40, Jesus commands us to love our neighbor as ourselves. Now, how can we love others properly if we do not love ourselves? I do not think that I can love others very well if I hate myself. It is my experience that the people who hate others with intensity hate themselves also. If God has commanded others to love us, then we should love and care for ourselves also. One of the ways to begin to love ourselves is to make sure that our boundaries are firmly in place. Setting and sticking to good boundaries is the first practical thing that we can do for ourselves. The main concept that we have to remember is that good self-esteem is not something that someone else will do for us, it is something we need to choose to do and choosing to have healthy self-esteem pleases God. What I am going to tell you next may surprise some people, and some of you will not even believe what I say, but please consider it because what I am about to tell you is one of the most powerful truths in the world. The simple truth is that, the more I praise God, the more fervent I praise God, the more I praise God in times of difficulty, the more self-esteem I have! Sounds impossible, I know, but I am telling you to try it because it works! Make sure you start your prayers with praise to Him, and praise Him through the day. Challenge yourself to do this for twenty-one days so it will become a habit. If you feel somewhat blue and your problems feel like the darkest night, it is the best time to praise Him. You will most likely feel much better as you praise Him in the night. And if it is easier to sing His praise, then by all means sing songs of praise, you are singing in the night and you will probably feel better as well as His presence with you giving you comfort. I have found that getting a really good picture of who God is and how He feels about us, helps the quest for good self-esteem better than anything. If you read through the whole book of Job, these passages give us a unique picture of God. The passages from chapters 38 to 41 give us a tiny look at the majesty, might, and awesome character of the Lord. Finding out just how amazing our God is helped me considerably because if the almighty Creator of the universe was interested in little old me, then I truly must have worth and value.

Action Plan and Assignment

1. Think about what Jesus has done for you and accept the fact that He would not have called you to Himself if you were not priceless.

2. Choose to accept and like the person that God created.

3. Review your boundaries and make sure they are in place.

4. Read Matthew 22:37–40.

5. Read Psalm 139.

6. Determine to pray for those who have hurt you, if you need to, make a list, and then pray for each person, pray for their salvation, enlightenment, and healing. This will actually bring about more healing to you than you can possibly imagine.

7. Read 1 Corinthians 3:16.

8. Read 1 Corinthians 6:19.

9. Read 2 Corinthians 6: 16.

10. Read Psalms of praise out loud, such as Psalm 148 and 149. Then praise our God for his beauty, love, intelligence, might, power, and all the things you know to be true about Him.

11. Make a list of the attributes of God and do a twenty-one-day praise challenge. Decide to begin each day and each prayer with praise for twenty-one days. By the end of the twenty-one days, praise will be a habit.

12. Make a firm decision to get to know God better. I firmly believe that the better we know Him, the better we feel about us.

13. Read Psalm 116.

14. Read Job 38–41.

Healing does not mean that the trauma and damage never occurred or existed, it means that the trauma can no longer control our lives—if we continue to live the manifestations of low self-esteem, it is one way that we continue to relive our past.

25

Self-Awareness

Learning the basics of how the enemy trips us up with negative self-esteem is one subject that we have talked about this in the last chapter. Having the ultimate self-esteem the way God intends you to is a continuance on the subject. I made the statement in a previous chapter, that when you get rid of a negative, you must replace the empty space with a positive. The previous chapter dealt with the combating the negative aspects of how the devil uses media and others to achieve his goal, now we can talk more about the positive and how to incorporate that into your life. How to have the self-esteem that God intended is relatively easy, but I must warn you that the devil will fight you on it every step of the way. You need to really be on your game here and use the Word of God with intent and purpose to defeat the devil's darts here. The good news is that the Bible tells us that when we resist the devil, he will flee from us, so eventually, as you practice the biblical concepts of good self-esteem, the devil will grow tired of fighting you and move on to someone else's easier target. Having good self-esteem is like all the other steps of healing in that self-esteem is a choice based on facts, not someone else's opinion. We can embrace good self-esteem when we believe what Jesus has done for us and how He feels about us.

> Are not 2 sparrows sold for a farthing? And one of them shall not fall on the ground without your Father. But the very hairs of your head are numbered. Fear ye not therefore, ye are of more value than many sparrows. (Matthew 10:29–31)

This passage is telling us that we are important to our Father in heaven. The scripture is saying that God even knows how many hairs we have on our heads! If our heavenly Father has taken the time to know how many hairs my head has, I must be loved indeed! I love my children more than life, but I have never taken the time to count their head hairs!

I think that the most important point here is that God is trying to let us know that we are important and that He loves us. We are chosen vessels and a treasure to Him. When we know that we are a treasure to our God, how can we feel bad about ourselves? Knowing the truth of how a holy God feels about us certainly can make the commercials that tell us we need their stuff to be acceptable seem rather silly. Salvation in Jesus Christ is basically believing and repenting. Positive self-esteem works the same way. First, we must in faith believe that we are loved by Him and valuable. Second, we must repent of all the bad stuff we bought into and know that He loves us.

I know that it sounds too simplistic, but faith in how God feels about us is really all that it takes. We all need to get it into our heads that the opinion of others has no merit here, it is only what God thinks that counts. Our God can be relied upon to correct us when we make mistakes, but his correction of us *never* changes His love for us. One day when I was noticeably irritated with Mark, our granddaughter, Adrianna, overheard. Adrianna asked me if Papa and I were getting a divorce.

I explained to her that Papa was not my favorite person just then, but I certainly was not going to divorce him. We all are irritated with those that we love at one time or another. I do not envy people who tell me that they never had a disagreement with their spouse, children, or friends, I just do not believe a word they say. I do not stop loving my family because they are not perfect, and God does not stop loving His family when they are not perfect either. We are a treasure to Him and it does not matter to Him what color our skin is or whether it is wrinkled or smooth.

He loves us just as much when we drive an old or new car or no car at all. He does not give us extra "points" because we bought our kids expensive shoes, had the "correct" body mass, played the perfect game, or set the perfect table.

God cares about our hearts. He cares about our love for each other, our honesty, integrity, and willingness to obey Him. But if we fall short of some of these things, as we sometimes do, He still loves us. Our focus should not be whether we have "perfect" (if there is such a thing) bodies, our focus should be on what we can do for the Lord today and how we can please Him.

When I am obsessed with earthy things, my self-esteem suffers because I will never be perfect in all the earthy things, but when I am obsessed with how I can please Jesus, my self-esteem blossoms because I am abiding in His love. When I finally set my focus on who He is and pleasing Him each day, the voices of self-loathing quieted down considerably.

> Whether therefore ye eat, or drink, or whatsoever ye do, do all to the glory of God. (1 Corinthians 10: 31)

We need to get our focus off of ourselves and on to Him, and then, as if by miracle, our self-esteems improve!

Starting and ending each day with scripture and prayer is a good start, but being mindful of Him every hour of the day makes every day go better and ultimately makes me feel better about me because I am in constant reminder of His love for me. Nothing that the Park Avenue executives try to sell us can compare with this feeling, once you finally get a proper dose of it. No mud that anybody has flung at us (past or present) can stick to us when we get a real picture of who we are and How wonderful our God is. Only God can judge us and He has the whole picture. Others who judge us only have a part of the truth, never the whole truth, because only God knows our hearts. Maybe that is one reason why God says in His Word that He is so annoyed with people who judge others, no one else has the right. Anyone who is going to judge you on the basis of your body size, skin color, where you live, what car you drive, whether or not you dishes have water spots, or even some wrong that they perceive you doing, elevates themselves to being equal with God. When have you ever met someone equal with God? There was only one person born who was equal with God and that is Jesus.

If you read the book of Revelation, you will plainly see that even the angels in heaven have no right to judge, only Jesus has that privilege. I have no idea if the apostle Peter struggled with low self-esteem while he was getting out of prison, but I doubt it.

The man made mistakes that are clearly documented in the Word of God for all of us to see. Poor guy, imagine your mistakes put down in print for others to know about for 2,000 years!

Whatever his thoughts are about his shortcomings being documented, I doubt that Peter suffered with low self-image because he clearly walked too close to God to be afflicted by negative self-image.

This is our formula for right self-image. When we get our hearts as close to God as we can be, when we love Jesus with all our hearts and minds, when we are more concerned with our "inner man" than our "outer man," then our self-esteem is more in tune with what the Lord wants for us. When we are more concerned about putting forth a Godly appearance before the world, we will not be tormented by what the world thinks of us. When we are more concerned about pleasing Jesus, horrific past traumas do not seem so significant.

Scripture commands us to love others as we love ourselves. If we do not love us, how can we obey God by loving others?

Action Plan and Assignment

1. Read Psalm 139:14.

2. Read Matthew 6:26 and Matthew 10:28–31.

3. Read Romans 8:1 and James 2:8.

4. Read and contemplate Matthew 5:43–44 and Matthew 7:1–6 learn to see that the judgment and opinions of other people have no merit on your self-worth; learn to know that God is not pleased when others judge you.

26

Sing at Night

It was actually quite late in life when I finally learned how to really obtain the peace and power of God with regularity. I think that all of us who have known great pain long for constant peace, joy, and pain-free nights. I think that the nighttime is when the insecurity is greatest. During the day, there are constant distractions. We are engaged in work, relationships, music, children, TV, housework, hobbies, mowing the lawn, shoveling the drive, choosing our gourmet coffee, looking at social network sites, news programs, even deciding what is for dinner can be a distraction from thinking about the negative things that life has bombarded us with. At night, just before we drift off to sleep, it is quiet and we have no distractions to give us comfort. In the night, it is just us. I think that is why the sleep aid industry is profitable. Instead of sleeping, the annoyances of the day manifest themselves and the pain of the past pays us a visit. It is not long before someone that is really tired after a full day is wide awake, trying to solve tomorrow's problems and yesterday's hurts. Again, the scriptures show us the answer to this dilemma. In the book of Acts 16, we read the true story of Paul and Silas in prison. It seems to me that God might do some of his greatest miracles when those he loves are in prison. We looked at Peter in prison and his miraculous escape, and as we who have known trauma were in a prison of pain, we have been looking at the miracle of healing that God, through Jesus can bring, if we but get up and follow. Sometimes, our actions need to be very active, like putting on our shoes and rising up, and sometimes, they are more subtle, but just as effective. In Acts 16, we are told that Paul and Silas were beaten and put into prison for spreading the Word of God and ministering to the people. After their beating, verse 24 of chapter 16 tells us that the pair was thrust into the inner prison (I suppose this means maximum security) and made their feet fast in the stocks. I suppose that If I was thrown into maximum security for doing good deeds and had my ankles in shackles, I might be very tempted to cry and wail to God, if for nothing more than I was sore from being beaten. In verse 25, the Bible says: "And at midnight Paul and Silas prayed, and sang praises unto God: and the prisoners heard them."

The Bible tells us that during the singing, there was a great earthquake and all the doors of the prison were opened. It also goes on to say that everyone's shackles were loosed. I know that all of this that happened was in the physical sense, but I think that there is also a spiritual application here. I must admit that I read over these passages of scripture a thousand times before I really got the message.

The message here is no matter what your circumstances, no matter how bad your circumstances, no matter how much pain you feel, no matter how black the night is, praise God. Singing is a great way to do it, but telling him words of appreciation, thanks, and praise will work just as well. It matters little how bad your circumstances were today, you can always find joy in your day and a reason to praise Him. And when you do, the shackles of the pain in your heart will be loosed.

If in this country we live in, with all our advantages and blessings, we cannot find things to praise and thank Him for, then it is not surprising if we cannot sleep. I started to deliberately find things to praise God about, just because I wanted to obey Him. I began to make it a habit to, several times a day, just praise Him for who He is. After just a few days of doing this, I was transformed! I had more energy, my spirits were lifted above the clouds, and I slept better. I should add here, that when I started my obedient praise days, it was some of the darkest days of my life. Circumstances were really bad and there was no indication that things would get better. Obediently praising God, however, is not contingent upon good circumstances. Paul and Silas did not have great circumstances when they sang and praised in prison, and neither did I. There were so many dark and frightening things in my life at that time, that although I did not feel as if I was in prison, I certainly was in a dark place. I felt as if I was in the dark of night. I felt as if it was almost as black as the day I was abducted. I had every good reason to be extremely depressed, and if I had consulted with some counselors, I am certain that they would have agreed with me. In view of my checklist of unfair happenings, unfair people, economic downturns, deaths that should not have happened, and a thousand other awful circumstances happening all at once, I had every right to be depressed, angry, and bitter. And then, just when I thought it could not get any worse, my car engine blew up.

I did not consult a psychologist, a preacher, or even a doctor to give me an antidepressant. I had been practicing the truths of praise consistently, but I had never been as enthusiastic about praise as I was as that point. I decided that in my dark night, I would sing and praise to God with more fervor and zeal, and I would mean it wholeheartedly. I decided to *truly* praise Him with everything in me over and over in the day and not fuss about my circumstances. There are hundreds of scriptures that tell us to praise God, but before that time, I had never taken them very seriously, I thought they were just nice flowery words. I had read probably as many commands of God, where He instructs people to praise him, and for most of my life I had ignored those too. When my daily life started to be so transformed by the simple acts of praise, I was really irritated with myself that I had not done it before. I could have saved myself a lot of misery. Going through the corridors of emotional prison and heading toward the iron gates would have been so much easier if I had just been praising Him then! Words really cannot adequately tell anyone how practicing praise has transformed my life. I could go on and on and say how circumstances do not matter, but no one would believe me unless they tried it for themselves. Another passage that illustrates the power of praise so well is 2 Chronicles 20 where we are told that the children of Israel are in another battle. 2 Chronicles 20–22 says that they rose early in the morning and Jehoshaphat told them just to believe God. He (Jehoshaphat) told the people that they should praise the beauty of holiness (which is the Lord) and he appointed singers and told the people to be in this mind as they went out to face the enemy. In verse 22, the scripture tells us:

> And when they began to sing and to praise, the Lord sent ambushments against the children of Ammon, Moab, and mount Seir, which came against Judah, and they were smitten.

I found that as I began my day with praise and gave Him gratitude and praise throughout the day that the Lord would send ambushments for my negative anxieties. The anxieties vanished and I had a new and renewed strength I am convinced that praising our God is the best treatment for anxiety and heartbreak. I cannot tell you why it works, I just know that it does. I was and still am enjoying peace, joy, and pain-free nights.

I wonder how often the negative aspects of everyday life, such as an unbelieving spouse, bad job, rebellious kids, chronic physical pain, crushed fenders, leaky roofs, lost jobs, and IRS audits, would be put to rest, if we just all learned the positive action of praising God and making it our daily practice. What would happen to our country, our world, our family, if we all just would sing in the night?

What kind of prison walls would come down, relationships heal, and finances flourish? I do not know the answer to that question because I think that we should praise God without expecting a reward, in fact, I think if we would "expect" some reward for praise it probably would not happen. God deserves our praise just because He is God. He created us, provided for us, and loved us. We (as a nation) have mostly complained, bickered, and whined, then we wonder why He does not give us more. I know that we should praise Him most during the bad times because Isaiah 61 tells us to put on the garment of praise for the spirit of heaviness. In other words, if you spirit is heavy, praise God and your spirits will be lifted. I have learned that singing in the night elevates us to walk in the light and keeps us from the sting of pain that the world might bring. Notice I did not say it would keep us from the pain, but from the sting of pain.

Action Plan and Assignment

1. Read Psalm 142:7.
2. Read Acts 16:16–34.
3. Read 2 Chronicles: 20:20–22.
4. Read Romans 8:28–34.
5. Read Isaiah 61:3.
6. Read Psalm 67.
7. Read Psalm 42:8.
8. Read Psalm 77:6.
9. Read Luke 6:12.

27

Cups of Water

If you have walked through the corridors and accomplished the work at each station, you are truly ready to begin on a marvelous journey of peace and prosperity of spirit. When we have completed all the tasks and begun to feel marvelous, the enemy comes to us to try and trip us up with the past again, lying to us and telling us that it is not over and that we are still in bondage to the hideous traumas that he brought us.

At this point, we have two choices:

1. We can decide that the devil is right, that we cannot possibly be healed. Then we beat ourselves up and tell ourselves what a failure we are. In doing this, we keep ourselves in the bondage of trauma, which is the devil's plan and we never completely accomplish the beautiful life that God wants for us, or

2. We combat the darts of the devil by getting out of ourselves. Realizing that it is not all about me. I can command the devil in the name of Jesus to leave me alone because I have completed the tasks and have been put on this earth to serve others and I am a part of the body of Christ, saved for good works.

Each of us has been put on this earth to accomplish good things, but if we stay blocked in the past, rolling it over in our minds again and again, then an abundance of good things that we are put here to do, do not get done and we miss out on blessings.

The most difficult thing that I have had to overcome is wanting to hide and be invisible. Because of the things I have endured, this is an understandable reaction and I have talked to countless survivors of trauma who struggle with the same problem. I would so much prefer to live out my days on my ranch, hours from the nearest city, rarely seeing anyone except friends and family, just enjoying the scenery, gardens, and animals of my life. I could feel happiness in my Lord God, then my husband, grandkids, colorful quilts, flowers, books, and everything lovely, being almost completely invisible to almost everyone else, picking and choosing all the safest, nicest, loveliest times, consequently, living all my life all for me! The above scenario is not God's plan or even His best for me. The Word says that we were saved unto good works and we are not to put our salvation light under a bushel (Mark 4:21) but on a candlestick to shine the light of God to everyone. Giving of ourselves to others is the rest of the story. I believe that there are many people with traumatic hurts who have never gone the distance through the prison corridors, meeting the gates, who feel better just because they give of themselves to others. I have learned that skipping these all important tasks and just getting to the giving part can leave us only partially healed, but I do know that giving without doing the rest can result in a fairly good life. I say this to show just how important to our well-being giving is, but do not shortchange yourself by leaving out the other steps. Do all that you can for the most complete healing. Remember in the first chapters you were asked just how healed you want to be. You were asked to decide if some pain is okay or do you want complete healing. Of course, complete healing requires the previous steps but giving to others gives us an extra blessing. Let me put it another way. As it relates to our complete healing, *giving is* the icing on the cake, the color in the flowers, the wag of the dog's tail, the baby's first smile, the warmth of a hug from a treasured friend, the colors in the sunsets, the thrill of winning the big game. All of the above things we can actually do without.

No one really needs to see the color in the flowers. We can all have a happy and normal life without them and thousands of other things, but these things make our life so much richer and nicer! It is the same with giving of ourselves. We all can function without it, but the acts of giving to others supplies a joy in us that nothing else can. When we choose to focus our giving on the things that are most important to the Lord, our joy intensifies to something that cannot even be defined. Jesus the Christ who owned everything in the universe chose to give it up for a season to come here and give to us His wisdom, His love, and ultimately His life. Jesus is our example. He wants us to give to Him and each other, believe it or not, not just for their sakes or His sake, but for our own joy and happiness.

There are tens of thousands of ways that we can be givers. Some people give as ministers of the gospel, Sunday school teachers, deacons, or choir directors and there are so many people that think these are the only ways that we can really give to God. May I suggest that these are only a few of the ways that we can give? May I also be so bold as to suggest that it is possible that some of the things we dismiss as insignificant and almost worthless to God can be some of the biggest things. There have been times at Thanksgiving when it was only Mark and I, no family, so we decided to celebrate Thanksgiving by volunteering at the local homeless shelter. I have served God before in my giving by bringing a meal to a sick person. Providing a ride to and from someplace important to the recipient. Taking time to listen to someone's tale of frustration and woe, then trying to give words of encouragement. When you are at the grocery checkout, being first to bid the checker a nice day is a marvelous giving gesture. Most of us have no real idea what some service industry people suffer from the public they serve. Anytime you are giving someone your love and understanding, you are a giver. The Word of God states in Mark 9:41 that if you just give a simple cup of water in the name of Jesus that you act of kindness will not go unnoticed. If your church is small, the people who clean it are probably unnoticed, but this is an act of giving that God will see and record.

The Bible says that if we give to others, it will be given to us good measure pressed down shaken together and running over (Luke 6:38). I have heard some preachers say that this means that you will prosper financially. In some cases, that may be, but I think that if you believe this scripture is only for your financial gain, you are missing the larger point. Some of the best gifts that God can bestow on us are not financial, but unless you are giving for His honor and glory, you will miss them because words cannot describe this kind of wealth.

Some of the blessings for our giving we will not receive till we see Him in glory and He rewards us then. Some of the blessings of our giving no one but us may never see because as we give and consider others, emotional healing is a byproduct. If we are truly giving of ourselves to please God and we are giving as a way to show Jesus gratitude for what He has done for us, we can expect to feel so much better. I do not know why humans are hardwired to give to others in order to get themselves blessings, but we are, and if this is the motivation to give, it is a selfish motivation. At my time of life, I think that I am qualified to comment on the *fact* that selfish people are the most miserable in the world. In their selfishness, they sometimes errantly think that if they obtain more stuff, they will be happy. Happiness never comes to these people because true happiness can never be found in stuff and sinful experiences. It is just not there. Without exception, I have never met a happy person who has lived their life selfishly. They might pretend to be happy in front of you, but if you spend enough time with them, you will see that their misery is without definition. Selfishness produces unhappy miserable people, and if you would read the biblical books of Lamentations, Proverbs, and Ecclesiastes, you would see that God says that selfishness produces unhappy people. If you were to do a biblical search of the stories of named characters in the Bible and were to read their stories you will find that the selfish characters always suffered negative consequences for their attitudes and actions.

I know from personal experience that the times in my life when I have been the most selfish, I have not been the most joyful. The *best* and most *rewarding* sacrifices we can make are the sacrifices of prayer and praise to our Holy and wonderful creator God. These again are the giving times that no one else might ever see, but these giving sacrifices are a sweet smelling savor to our Lord. I am reminded of Luke 2:36–38 where a certain woman has been immortalized in scripture for her prayers and fasting alone. The first time I read these passages, the phrase about Anna that she "served God with fastings and prayers night and day" has left an enormous impact on my life. The scripture here shows just how important "giving" your time to honor God is valued with Him. I do not think that we honor Him enough in church or privately with our prayers. We do not pray and glorify Him as we should. Mostly we, as a whole, sing in church (the time we are suppose to be glorifying Him with our voices), with half-hearted words, looking as if we have all just sucked a very sour lemon. I know that there are exceptions. I am talking about the majority of activity in our churches that are supposed to be the times set aside for worship.

We are suppose to be glorifying His name, not thinking we wish they would get on with it and get to the sermon, which we hope will be uplifting for us (notice the selfishness). We think about us when we are suppose to be worshiping Him, then we wonder why we do not get our short (can't take too much time, things to do, God will understand) prayers answered. Before you think that I am being judgmental to all, you need to know that these are issues I had to deal with in my own life. I asked God to show me why my prayers were not being answered in the ways I would like, and He showed me that I was not worshiping and giving in the way He would like. I learned then and there that giving to God in prayers, fastings, and adoration is the most important giving of all. This is why singing His praises when our life seems black as a moonless night is more helpful to healing than anything that any counselor, psychologist, psychiatrist, or even preacher can offer. Mark and I learned this together and we asked God to forgive us for the selfishness that used to be the norm of our life. We learned the benefit of turning off the TV and giving Him time. We still watch some TV, we now are just more conscious of how much we watch verses how much time we have spent with our Lord. We are not as unbalanced as we used to be. We learned the benefit of eliminating certain people, places, programs, and amusements that might not glorify God. We were not into anything that the Bible would call evil or improper, but we became more aware and even though something might not be considered "bad," we now wonder if we could make a better choice, something that would give God pleasure. It is just a matter of becoming aware of the things we might give God, instead of our own amusements.

When we begin to feel the great freedom that a healed body enjoys, we must realize that there was a long time when the fear, anger, and misery of the trauma filled our lives. When all the fear, anger, and other aspects of the trauma are gone, it creates a hole. The absences of the horror creates in us a vacuum that we need to fill with a positive. That positive is giving. Giving is the plug for the hole that healing has created.

Giving to God and serving Him first should be everyone's normal day. Giving our tithes are another way we give to God. Jesus sacrificed His whole life and dignity for us is the 10 percent that God requires really so much? After all, the government is taking much more than 10 percent. I have always been a bit irritated by that if 10 percent is good enough for God, then why does the US government think it needs more?

The whole point of this lesson is to learn to give to God in that you are gifted in. Sometimes, giving to others in creative ways is a way to give to God, but always need to remember to serve Him with our prayers and adoration first of all.

Action Plan and Assignment

1. Read Mark 4:21.
2. Read Mark 9:41.
3. Read Luke 6:38.
4. Read Acts 20:35.
5. Read James 2:14–18.
6. Read 2Corinthians 9:7.
7. Read Malachi 3:8.
8. Find and list personal ways for you to be a giver.

28

On Guard

As you grow in the newness of your newfound power and healthy self-esteem, there will be ways that can become pitfalls to your better life and trip you up along the way. If you remember a few simple principles and scriptures, you will not be as likely to fall back into subconsciously letting yourself renew your old victim mentality. Refer back to the chapter on "Know Your Enemy" if you have to, but always remember that the devil is a roaring lion (1 Peter 5:8–9) seeking whom he may devour and he knows all your weaknesses. Because you have been a victim in the past and displayed victim mentality, such as poor self-esteem and lack of boundaries to name just two, the devil knows that you might be weak in these areas and may strike you there again. Never underestimate his evil ways. The devil can use any people who choose to be his willing participant in tripping you up and putting you back into the bondages of anger, unforgiveness, lack of boundaries, or negative self-image. Recently, Mark and I were discussing a sermon we heard in church based on Colossians 3:10–17. The preacher was highlighting the parts of scripture that relate to how we should treat one another. I heard nothing amiss in the pastor's message and thought it was well presented and so did my husband. I did however find a part of the preacher's message that could confuse the healing in a survivor of trauma. It was not what he said, but what was omitted. The preacher is young and, thank the Lord, has probably never been a trauma survivor, so these are not things he would generally be sensitive to. Because the congregation is large, I am sure that there are many many survivors in this church and probably most of them have never talked to the pastor about their ordeals. I find that most survivors just do not want to discuss their past with too many people and some never tell the horrors at all, so I am sure that he never thought to venture down certain particular paths of dialogue. Yes, it is true that we are to forbear one another, forgive one another, refrain from quarrels, and be longsuffering, humble, and meek. We are supposed to treat one another with kindness, compassion, and humility, esteeming the other person above ourselves. Unfortunately, when we are not looking or paying full attention, the devil can use these very strengths of character in us to make us victims all over again, simply because we are giving these gifts of kindness to someone who intends to do us harm. If we are not careful, we can allow someone who does not love God (but pretends to love Him) to hurt us again. Maybe not in the same way we were victimized before, but hurting just the same simply because we were following the principles of God and someone took advantage of our goodness. It is *always* right to follow biblical principles even if it is painful to us. It is also always okay to recognize the manipulations of unscrupulous people. It is always okay to walk away from those people who intend us harm, and just because they are regular church attendees, give lots of money, teach Sunday school or other worthy things does not mean that they are safe, reliable, or honest.

Think of Judas when he betrayed Jesus. Jesus told the disciples that there was one with a devil among them, but none of the disciples knew who it was! Judas acted like the rest, talked like the rest, casted out demons like the rest, and was the treasurer who was entrusted with all the money for the group. Judas was evil and no one suspected. Unfortunately, the devil might plant some of these people among us to mess up not only our lives, but the lives of others, but if we recognize the tactics the damage will be minimal or nonexistent. We are not helpless, but we must be vigilant.

Let me remind you that when you have been a victim of a serious incident, oftentimes, you will recognize the same type of person who traumatized you even before you are introduced. It is very common for those of us who have suffered so horrifically to be uncomfortable with certain people and not know why. Ask yourself if you have ever been uncomfortable or frightened with a person and you really have not gotten to know him. Everyone says that he/she is so nice. I can honestly say that 100 percent of the time when I have been ill at ease with someone, time has proved to me that I was right in not trusting him/her. If you are uncomfortable, frightened, or uneasy with someone you have just met, listen to your instincts and pray about the situation fervently. I also know for a fact that however you have been violated, the devil remembers and can send other abusers to you to step all over your rights as a human being. I have talked to countless numbers of survivors who bear out this fact asking me why they keep attracting dirt bags to themselves. They sometimes go from one job and relationship to another, constantly picking the same types of "friends," love relationships, bosses, and situations and always wondering how another unscrupulous person masquerading as a Christian found them again. Again, I say, your first clue is that you are uneasy. You cannot put your finger on it, but you are uneasy. You are *not* violating Colossians 3 if you put your guards and your radar up. Something is wrong, do not give your trust away, this person has not earned it, and you are uncomfortable. I think that God, through the Holy Spirit, gives us the gift of fear, but sometimes, we are too nice to listen to it. Listen to it, this is your early warning sign. I have heard it said by someone that when somebody shows you who they are the first time believe them. The second way to protect yourself is to stop making excuses for someone else's bad behavior. Yes, we should treat even bad people like Colossians 3 tells us, but do not ignore the facts. The fact is, if someone is critical of others, what makes you think they will not be critical of you?

The fact is, if you catch someone in a lie, how can you believe that they are not a liar? The fact is if someone refuses to respect your personal space, why do you think they are not abusive? My pet peeve is when I tell someone that I do not wish to be embraced, called, addressed, or visited, they do it anyway. To me, that is a red flag that I am dealing with a manipulating selfish person who has no regard for the needs and feelings of others and does not respect me. These people are controllers and it is my experience that a controller *never* has my best interest or rights at heart, even though they say they that they do. The fact is, if someone hurts the feelings of another then excuses it instead of apology and repentance, expect them to be insensitive again. The fact is, that you cannot believe what someone says they are, you need to look at their actions. If their words do not match their actions believe their actions not their words. I get very wary of someone who talks about God all the time but is oblivious to the feelings and rights of others. Colossians 3:10–17 is all about respecting the feelings and rights of others. Now, when someone blatantly and continuously violates the principals of Colossians 3 where I am concerned, I feel I have the right to temporarily be angry at their insensitivity. (Notice I said temporarily, or shortly, not continuously.) I tell them that it is not okay to treat me like this. then I wait for the apology, which is not really needed as I have already forgiven them, but the apology is needed to let me know they agree that the behavior was not okay and will not happen again.

When Mark and I were discussing this, we had a slight disagreement. Mark pointed out that as the preacher pointed out, Colossians 3: 15 says we should do all as Christ did. If Jesus would not do it, then we should not do it. Mark further stated that Jesus did not get angry with people so we should not either. This is not a wrong statement, I just did not think it was complete. My reply was to remind him that Jesus went into the temple and overthrew the money changers and certainly was acting more angrily than meekly in that situation (Matthew 21:12–13 and Mark 11:15–17).

"True," Mark agreed, "but those people were desecrating the temple." I replied with 1 Corinthians 3:16–17 and 6:19–20 which tells us that if Christ is our savior, then our bodies are the temple of the Holy Spirit. The Word says that now God's temple is not a temple made with hands. If we love Jesus and are born again (John 3) then we are the temples of the living Holy Spirit. Is it okay not to desecrate a temple made with hands but quite all right to desecrate the temple of the Holy Spirit? In summary, there are some times in life when try as you might, someone will not respond correctly to the teachings of Colossians 3. That does not mean we should not practice the principles. We should always practice the principles of Colossians 3 even if the other person is not so kind, but in most cases, we can walk away from a person who does not abide by those principles or not get into a relationship with them in the first place. If we apply principles of protection such as determination not to get into a relationship except for praying for certain people, then we probably will never be tempted to be angry with them. When I have been angry with them, it has been for a short time, and sometimes, I do not get angry at all even when challenged with a really tough situation. I pray about it and know that God will work it out for me and I know that it is not His perfect will that I get entangled with this person in business, friendship, or anything else. I can be polite and I can pray for them, but I do not have to let them desecrate my temple in word or deed.

What I think that God wishes for you to take away here is to believe and know that you are valuable and He is just as upset with people desecrating your temple as Jesus was two thousand years ago when some desecrated the stone temple. Because He is not pleased to have your temple spoiled, I know that He wishes us to be aware and practice careful observation before entangling ourselves with others. Here are some negative character traits that you should be aware of and possibly need to protect yourself from.

1. Controlling personality. This is someone who insists that they are always right and you are always wrong. This type will not take no for an answer and is insistent that you think their way and do their way. When you say no to a controlling personality, they are likely to argue with you for hours or months and years until they wear you down and you give in. If wearing you down with their words does not produce the result they want, they may bring someone else into the fight for your compliance.

2. Manipulative personality. This personality is a direct offshoot of the controller. A manipulator does not usually show his/her face unless their talk and the talk of others has failed, so this one is difficult to recognize unless you observe this type manipulating someone else. If you ever observe someone manipulating another person with words or actions, it may be time to exit the stage, you may be in total agreement with them now, but in the future, if you disagree, you will be expected to bow down and accept the manipulator's way.

3. Selfish personality. This one can be *very* hard to detect because very often the selfish person looks like a generous one. Whenever I come into contact with someone who is giving money, time, and goods freely and letting *everyone* know about their generosity, a red flag goes up in my mind. Every time I have encountered a person that loves to get their checkbook out and shower me with gifts, I have found that these "gifts" are not free and not gifts at all. Too often, someone that is seemingly generous with their money and or time will call in the favor later. This also is a controller. This type of person will remind you in a second what they did for you when they want something

that you find dishonest, unfair, or not in your best interest to do. The Bible says not to let your right hand know what you left hand is doing. In other words, a truly unselfish person will not be so flamboyant.

4. Narcissist personality. This type of personality is the epitome of selfishness. A narcissist always needs to be the center of attention. I have actually come across a couple of preachers that fit this description. Most pastors are loving, humble servants not worthy of this tag, but it is always in your best interest to look closely at everyone and remember that they are also looking closely at you. A narcissist is always looking for the best way that he/she can use you to his/her advantage. The needs of others are never as important as their wants, no matter how trivial the wants may be. A narcissist seems unable to feel the feelings of others and usually is unsympathetic. I had a run-in with this type of personality a while ago. She gives money like she has a tree in her backyard, always is looking to be the center of attention, talks about God constantly when she is not talking about herself, and decided that because she could not control me (I do not, in her opinion, possess all of her fine qualities) that I am unworthy of my husband. This woman set out on a quest to win Mark's affection and thereby save him from the clutches of the woman (me) that in her mind is totally unworthy of such a great guy! I guess in her mind that would make adultery okay in God's book. However, she had one *big, big* problem: the problem was that Mark loves me and let her know in more than one way that he was not interested in her. This did not go well with her (she made trouble for me), so Mark made the decision not to be anywhere where she could annoy me further. We changed churches.

5. Critical personality. This one is actually very easy to identify. If you are around someone that is constantly

critical of others, you should wonder what this person says about you when you are not around. A critical personality can easily plunge you right back into a victim mentality even if they are not trying to do so.

6. Angry personality. We all get angry about something sometime. We need to pick our battles carefully. Most of us can easily decide when to just let it go and realize that the subject at hand is really not worthy of an argument or a blood pressure elevation. An angry personality does not seem to distinguish which thing to get angry about. They are angry about everything. People get angry when the thing happening is not their way. I know this to be true, and if you think about it for a few minutes, you will probably agree that every time an anger response welled up in you, it was because things were not going your way. The garage mechanic promised your car today but says it will be next week, you order food in a restaurant and it comes to you cold and tasteless, someone promised to be there to help you with the bazaar but has changed her mind, your child treats you with disrespect, your boss treats you with disrespect, the mail delivers your package broken, you get rear-ended, you get cheated out of some money, you become traumatized and victimized because another person was selfish. There are hundred more reasons why someone might get angry, but a true angry personality does not need a reason, they are just angry all the time. You can always tell if the person you are talking to has a chronic angry personality with one question. Ask him/her why he/she is angry. A person with a chronic angry personality will get red in the face, scream at you, and angrily insist that they are not angry! Proverbs 22:24 says, "Make no friendship with an angry man; and with a furious man thou shalt not go."

7. Proud personality. "God resisteth the proud, and giveth grace to the humble" (1 Peter 5:5). It has been my experience that proud people have always led me into uncomfortable situations.

8. Lying personality. When you catch someone in a lie the first time, pay attention. You should avoid the above kinds of people and all the situations if you possibly can. If some think that I am being too critical of others, that I should be more tolerant of these imperfections, and they would say, "After all, we are all human and sinners," let me answer with this: "These 6 things doth the Lord hate: yea, seven are an ABOMINATION unto Him: A proud look, a lying tongue, and hands that shed innocent blood. An heart that deviseth wicked imaginations, feet that be swift in running into mischief, A false witness that speaketh lies, and he that soweth discord among brethren (Proverbs 6:16–19).

Action Plan

1. Read Colossians 3:10–17. Determine that this is how you will treat others, but decide that you also should be treated in this manner by others.

2. Read 1 Corinthians 3:16–17 and 1 Corinthians 6:19–20.

3. Read John 7:24.

4. Consider this chapter as a further commentary on "Boundaries."

5. Value yourself, you are precious to God and so are others, even unscrupulous people, but we do not have to give them permission to disrespect us. When they do this, it is not keeping with Colossians 3.

Pray for those who hurt you.

Thinking about a need to forgive God sounds blasphemous to most people. God is holy and righteous, and he has done no wrong, so when would there ever be a need to forgive the almighty God who crated the heavens and earth?

Almost every survivor of trauma and anyone who has suffered the death of a loved one gets mad at God. Anger at God during times of duress is common, but is never a right attitude to live your life by. Because anger toward God is usually part of the feelings and issues that people deal with, I thought I needed to address the subject. God has never done anything wrong and he is always perfect, but on a subconscious level, a survivor might feel anger and hostility toward God for allowing the trauma. A survivor can sometimes wonder where the guardian angels were when he/she was going through so much pain. A survivor acknowledges that his/her life was spared, but questions why he/she had to endure it in the first place. Where was my God? Why didn't he protect me? What did I do to deserve this? The questions may be endless but the conclusion is often anger toward God, even if we do not consciously recognize it. Any therapist will tell you that anger toward God is a common occurrence after a major trauma. Unfortunately, some survivors have stayed angry with God for so long that it becomes a part of the personality of the survivor and even considered the normal part of the person. He is a big God, He can take it, but if we are to finally walk through the iron gates of emotional freedom, we must deal with this in a Godly manner. Pretending that you are not angry with God will not solve your problem if you really are angry deep down inside. The root of such an attitude is the belief that "I am entitled to never have pain or sorrow." None of us has the right to demand or expect such an entitlement. Some earlier discussions were about moving on, forgiving, and letting go of the people and circumstances that have caused such grief. In my personal struggle, I had felt like God let me down. Where was he when a little innocent girl was being taken away and her life changed forever? Where were my guardian angels? Why did he let them do this to me? What about the other children? Why did he let the abuse of countless innocent children go on for so many years? Why didn't he just step in and make them all have heart attacks or something similar, so that I could get away? Why didn't the Lord God of the universe protect me? The facts seem to contradict themselves. How can a loving, forgiving, almighty Father allow such horrors? Was he out to lunch? I struggled with this for many years, keeping myself in the prison, seeing the gates opening, but unable to completely walk through the gates. Sorting these questions out took considerable time and intense effort, even if the answer was simple. I had to forgive God.

Remember, forgiveness is getting a right heart with God. Forgiveness is trusting God and letting the negative attitudes go. I had to let the feelings of questioning and betrayal go. God did not betray me, he did nothing evil or wrong, and it is what it is. I live in a sinful world. Mankind has a free will to do good or evil. If God stepped in and stopped all evil, then mankind no more has free will, but is a puppet. I am not the only survivor in the world. I remembered the stories of the Holocaust and thought about countless people murdered by serial killers. My daughter, Joy, has a law degree. She served in her county as the assistant DA and has prosecuted many criminals. When Joy was in law school, she related to me something from one of her classes. She gave me some statistics that I wish I had never heard. At the time that Joy was in law school, they told her that 80 percent of murders in this country never have an arrest! I was appalled to learn that most people get away with murder. I was so shocked about this that I questioned whether she was actually listening in class correctly. Joy informed me that I had been watching too many murder mysteries on TV that always bring the bad guy to justice within an hour! She also reminded me that an arrest does not always result in a conviction. Quite a wakeup call for me! Evil does happen in the world. I am not responsible for the evil that others do, but I am responsible for how I react to it. As I struggled to properly accept and absorb these concepts, I was reminded of an old fairy tale. In the old fairy tale of Sleeping Beauty, the wicked witch put a curse on the girl that said she would prick her finger on a spindle and die. The three good fairies come to the rescue of Sleeping Beauty. They said that they could not take back the witch's spell, but they could change the outcome. Sleeping Beauty would not die, but sleep till true love's kiss awakened her. Now, I know for a fact that wicked witches do exist, after all, one helped abduct me, but I do not believe in fairies, true love's awakening kiss, and all the other nonsense about spells and such, but the idea of changing an evil act into a thing of beauty is certainly biblical.

The Bible is full of stories of how evil came into people's lives, but when the people were surrendered to God, he helped them to use the evil circumstances, not only to bless them, but for the good of others also. God can turn all the ashes of our traumas into beautiful gardens. It takes time to process the hurt, but the secret to forgiveness is to know that God will work it all (even the evil we suffer) for good, even our good, if we surrender to him I had a difficult time thinking that God would just step back and watch me suffer, but sometimes even in our own lives, we need to step back and not rush in and rescue everyone from difficult situations. I can illustrate what I mean by telling a story that happened on our ranch one fine summer day. Our granddaughter, Adrianna, seems to have been born with the country running with the blood in her veins. Adrianna spends her summers with us, indulging her love of horses and country life. Our Adrianna has been on a horse since she was nine months old when Mark would place her on his saddle in front of him and walk around the place. The years have gone by and Adrianna has come a long way from riding double with Papa Mark. She has learned to care for, ride, and even has saddle broke her own horse. One July day, I was busy in my studio and lost track of a lot of time before I realized that I had not seen Adrianna in a long while. I walked outside to investigate and there saw our granddaughter with Freckles Fancy Annie (one of our best mares) tied next to the tack room, saddled, and ready to go. The rules on this ranch had been pretty simple, that is, horses are not to be taken out and ridden off the ranch unless Mark or I are present. Adrianna's determination was so complete that she even had the foresight to catch the stallion and move him to a safer location, so he could not annoy her as she rode Freckles. Adrianna informed me that she would not ride into the arena, but anywhere she wished, reminding me that she had recently rode this horse out with Papa Mark to help move our cattle herd.

I decided that maybe it was good to let her exercise a little self-confidence. After all, at the age of thirteen, every young girl should have every opportunity to feel confident and powerful within herself. I decided to let her ride out but cautioned her to stay on the ranch and not to leave under any circumstances. I explained to Adrianna that Freckles knew every inch of the ranch and was comfortable within its boundaries. I continued to explain to her that Freckles was extremely "buddy sour." Buddy sour is a term we use to describe a horse that does not wish to be away from the rest of the herd. I warned Adrianna that if the mare was taken too far away from the herd that she would panic. Freckles would be testy and hard to handle and may even be dangerous. I reminded her that Papa had not had time to work with Freckles so that she would be confident off the ranch. Adrianna nodded in agreement and then mounted the mare like a pro and headed north down our long driveway. At the end of the drive, instead of turning back onto the property, she headed west and kept going. I think I stopped breathing right then. I made a fast decision not to interfere with Adrianna's decision. I rushed into the house, grabbed a pair of binoculars, placed myself on the porch swing, and proceeded to watch her ride. For a while, the ride was uneventful, then in horror, I watched Freckles bolt and run twice, jump, twirl, and jump some more. She bolted again with determination, and I knew that the mare would be difficult, as she was in the prime of her life and a very fast runner. I started for the car, all the while praying. I was quickly going to drive down to this pair of "rodeo" entertainment and rescue my Adrianna. The voice of the Holy Spirit stopped me—wait. I raised the binoculars again and waited. This horse was giving my granddaughter a fight that would challenge any experienced horseman Then I noticed that Adrianna was handling the situation like a pro. I watched her sit correctly, hands perfect, and seat secure. She was putting Freckles through a series of turns and circles that Mark had taught her to do when a horse begins to challenge you. She was doing fine. The mare carried her closer and closer to our north gate. I did jump into my car then and quickly drove down to the edge of the driveway and closed the north gates. I knew that when Freckles saw the open gate that she would bolt again. Adrianna questioned me when she came to the gate, and I instructed her to take the mare down another half mile and turn her into the east gate. The pair passed the north gate and Freckles calmed down, as I predicted she would. She calmly carried Adrianna around and through the east gate, down the lane, through the yard, and back to the tack room. Adrianna slipped off and tied the mare and exclaimed, "Boy, Grandma, Papa was right! This horse is so fast she can poke a hole in the wind!" I began to breathe again. That summer, we saw something good happen in our Adrianna. We saw her confidence build and blossom. I think that letting her handle some tough situations (like the Freckles incident) made her feel more powerful within herself. We can't take all the credit, her mother is a good role model in that respect, and this same year, Adrianna tried and succeeded at other things that were difficult. As we walk through life, we are all faced with many challenges. Some are small, like Adrianna's riding incident, and some are large, like being kidnapped. When Adrianna was fighting with the mare, I was watching.

When I was abducted, God was watching. My choice not to interfere with Adrianna's problem resulted in her having more confidence and being a stronger person. God's choice not to immediately stop the people before they could hurt me has been more difficult to accept. It has also been more difficult for me to see any good come from it, but good has come. As I look back on my life and all of my struggles, hardships, and trauma, I pray and ask God to never let me go through those things again. I do not enjoy hard times and I do not like pain. When I see so many good things now, that I possess, things that probably would not have come to pass had I not gone through that horrible kidnapping, I can truly praise God with enthusiasm.

The only thing from this life that we will take into the next is the character that we build here on earth. I have lived long enough to observe that the strongest and best character traits almost always come out of the darkest moments of our lives, that is, if we respond correctly and courageously.

When dark moments and traumas arrive, we have a choice. We can choose to let it destroy us with anger, hate, unforgiveness, and depression *or* we can choose to respond to it with strength, love, mercy, understanding, grace, and forgiveness. One way destroys us, the other makes us beautiful.

I also used my experience to learn and gain truth. I learned truth about some things that some people question. I learned that Satan and demons exist and are in the world trying to hurt us. This is the primary truth of good and evil. I have seen demons and I know that there is no such thing as a "good" witch. The Bible tells us these truths and I also know them as facts. During my ritual abuse, they kept blaspheming the name of Jesus Christ. Because I heard this and because they were evil, I knew that anything they were chanting about Jesus was a lie. The whole ritual was one lie after another, totally mocking and hating God.

Their scheme backfired. Everything that the devil and his evil helpers did to me only made me want the goodness of God more.

When someone opened the Bible and showed me how I could have a personal relationship with Jesus, it did not take much persuasion. I wanted Jesus because I knew evil personally and understood the wages of sin well at the tender age of five. Would I have made this choice had I not been kidnapped? Maybe not. Many of the blessings in my life have been a direct result of how I reacted to my childhood trauma. That is, when I learned to react in a biblical way. Like the Sleeping Beauty fairy tale mentioned earlier, God did not take away my experience, but he changed it as only he can do. I chose to do what God asked, and he did for me the things I was incapable of doing for myself. I began to walk through to the iron gates of emotional freedom, and I can say, for all of you who have not yet made all the choices to obey God, concerning the healing steps, it is wonderful over here.

The previous story of Adrianna's struggle is tiny compared to real trauma and hurt, but the results can be the same, if we make the right choices. Your healing is more attainable than you think because healing is a choice, or rather, a series of biblical choices we are all capable of making. God will do the rest. Many years ago, when I was in therapy, struggling through the anger, depression, confusion, pain, and all the steps of grief and loss, I *never* thought I would be grateful for my abduction. Today I can honestly say that I am thankful for the trauma that I endured. I have no more pain, just scars, and scars are only reminders, not painful. I can use my scars in any way God wishes to try and help bring healing to others and to bring them to the truth of Jesus and bring glory and honor to His name.

When you are in the midst of the fighting for your life, your focus is so intensely fixed on the struggle that you cannot possibly see any potential good. I think that another reason we need to revisit the story of Peter in prison is to remind us that, yes, there is a struggle, but the gates are ahead. In the middle of the struggle, when I allowed myself to get a clear picture of the gates, I could be glad that God did not remove me from the trauma. May I encourage you to get a clear picture of the gates?

I can now see in so many ways how the abduction was meant by evil people to destroy me, but God turned it all around for my good and his glory.

The abduction is part of me, part of my story, but it did not define me, it is not who I am. My trauma was much more than pricking my finger on a spindle, and I am grateful that Jesus came to me to change the outcome.

Instead of death, I have life. The word of God tells us that all things work together for good to those who love God (Romans 8:28). I know this to be true.

What was meant for my destruction has turned out to be one of my greatest blessings. I am beginning to think that maybe the greatest overcomers might get the greatest rewards. Time will tell on this one, but in the meantime, if the days of our lives are the darkest night, we should sing in the night. The joy is in the Lord, He inhabits our praise, and He is always closer to us when we sing in the night. Thou hast proved my heart, thou hast visited me in the night (Psalm 17:3).

The author, Pamela R Garin, is available
for speaking engagements.
If your organization is interested, please see the website,
Pamelargarin.tateauthor.com

CPSIA information can be obtained
at www.ICGtesting.com
Printed in the USA
FSOW02n1015180716
22858FS